How to Say
NO
to Your Toddler

How to Say
NO
to Your Toddler

**Creating a Safe, Rational, and Effective Discipline
Program for Your 9-Month-Old to 3-Year-Old**

WILL WILKOFF, M.D.

BROADWAY BOOKS
NEW YORK

PRINTED IN THE UNITED STATES OF AMERICA

BROADWAY BOOKS and its logo, a letter B bisected on the
diagonal, are trademarks of Random House, Inc.

Visit our website at www.broadwaybooks.com

First edition published 2003

Book Design and Illustration by Lisa Sloane

Library of Congress Cataloging-in-Publication Data
Wilkoff, William G.
How to say no to your toddler : creating a safe, rational, and
effective discipline program for your 9-month-old to 3-year-old / by
Will Wilkoff.– 1st ed.
p. cm.
ISBN 0-7679-1274-8
1. Toddlers. 2. Infants. 3. Discipline of children. 4. Discipline of
infants. 5. Parenting. 6. Parent and child. I. Title.

HQ774.5.W55 2003
649'.64–dc21   2003048022
3 5 7 9 10 8 6 4 2

To my parents,
who gave me the freedom to explore
and the limits to keep me safe.

WILL WILKOFF, M.D.

Contents

chapter 3

Using "No" and Other Ways to Manage Behavior Effectively 49

chapter 4

Putting Your Plan to Work 123

chapter 5

Conclusion: Plan C 215

Index 223

The Importance of
NO

Do I Need THIS BOOK?

We arrive at the threshold of parenting with our own unique collection of strengths and vulnerabilities. All children are not cut from the same cloth, and each of us must adopt a parenting style that is appropriate for our child's age and personality. The possible combinations of child temperaments and parental personalities are so numerous that no author can claim to offer advice that will work in every situation, or a strategy that every parent will find appealing.

However, during my thirty years as a general pediatrician working with thousands of families, I have noticed that the parents who are successful at managing their children's inevitable misbehaviors have one thing in common. Whether they be lobstermen or college professors, they discover how to say "No" while their children are still toddlers. It wasn't always easy. They shared their struggles with me and together we worked out the solutions. Here are a few of their most frequently encountered scenarios. If some of them sound familiar, then you will find the answers you are looking for in this book.

When I say "No" my toddler laughs and runs away. You have been playing games with your child for months. Now he has to learn that there are situations when you mean business.

My partner and I disagree on how we should respond when our child misbehaves. Consistency is an important element in managing your child's behavior. However, it is only natural that sometimes the two of you will disagree about discipline. There are several ways to incorporate these expected inconsistencies into your approach to parenting.

Our daycare provider complains that our child is being too aggressive. If his behavior doesn't improve, we may be asked to find another daycare. In this era when two-earner families have become the norm, behavior management is not just something to be done at home. There are simple solutions to this complex issue.

I find myself screaming at my toddler to get him to behave. It seldom works and I don't like the way I sound. You can learn to use your words and your actions to manage your child's misbehaviors without raising your voice.

I'm embarrassed to admit that I have smacked my child's hand to stop a behavior. You knew it was a mistake the moment you did it, but under the circumstances you felt you were out of options. There are ways to change the circumstances and there are other, safer strategies that work.

I have read that I should be redirecting my toddler and providing positive reinforcement for his good behavior, but I've tried and he continues the same misbehaviors. While these two strategies can be components of a successful behavior management plan, without a coexisting set of consequences for misbehavior they are seldom effective. This book will show you how to draw age-appropriate limits and administer safe, humane, and effective consequences.

We've tried time-out, but it didn't work. Time-out still remains the safest and most effective way to discourage your child's misbehaviors, but many parents, like yourselves, must learn the fine points of the process before it will be effective.

I've listened to some parents who try to talk their child into behaving properly. These discussions sound silly and don't stop the misbehavior. It is very important to talk to your child and consider the motivations for his behaviors, but eventually you must stop discussing the situation and take action. There are safe and humane ways of moving beyond the words when the situation demands action.

Our child seems to come by her good behavior naturally, but we want to be prepared for the time when she begins to test us. You may have been blessed with a child who—for the moment—seems to require neither limits nor consequences. But, as you suspect, the bubble will burst someday. This step into the real world will be much easier if you already have a plan.

This book does not dictate a monolithic plan that must be followed in painful detail from A to Z to achieve success.

It is a collection of observations gathered over thirty years of watching thousands of parents succeed and fail at behavior management. I have arranged its chapters in what I consider to be a logical sequence, but you are encouraged to jump around and read the chapters that sound most appropriate first.

Whether it be the employment of earlier bedtimes, setting more age-appropriate limits, or learning how to use time-out, I am sure you will find the ingredients from which you can create an effective behavior management strategy that will fit your family's unique situation.

I have tried to keep this book short enough to be read in one or two evenings. From experience, I know that some chapters will need to be reread several times as new challenging behaviors erupt. I hope you find what I have to say helpful. If you do, please share what you have learned with other parents. Raising children is hard work and we all need a little encouragement from time to time.

BEHAVIORAL REALIST OR REALISTIC BEHAVIORIST? A book reviewer once described me as a behaviorist, and I guess if I were forced to crawl into a well-recognized psychological niche, the sign over the pigeonhole would read "Behavioral Therapist." I believe that we can mold behavior with positive and negative reinforcement, but if I could choose my own label, I would prefer to be known as a "Realist."

What you will read in this book is not based on theory, but on real world experiences. The most valuable portion of my education in child psychology began during my last year in medical school, when the first of our three children was born. Over the next thirty years, as I watched her and more than five thousand other children grow into adulthood, I observed what worked and what didn't work for my wife and myself and the other parents who were kind enough to share their experiences with me. I understand the challenges of parenting a toddler from firsthand experience. I won't ask you to make changes in your style that I haven't tried myself or seen other parents use successfully. I have realistic expectations for what you can accomplish, just as I want you to have realistic expectations for your child's behavior. You can be sure that although my advice may have a behavioral flavor it will always be realistic.

Now Is the Time to Learn How to Say "NO!"

IT ISN'T TOO EARLY. Your toddler has been capable of understanding that "No" means "Stop that behavior!" since he was at least nine months old and probably long before that. But like many parents, you may have been reluctant to give him credit for understanding your admonitions. After all, he's only a baby.

On the other hand, you may have been far more lenient in interpreting his ability to grasp your encouraging words. You have been talking to your baby from the first moment you saw his heart beating on a sonogram. You had been asking him questions, telling him stories, and sharing your emotions with him for many months before you saw an obvious response flicker across his face.

Although you may have erroneously given him credit for a grin before he was a week old, by six weeks of age he was definitely smiling in response to your foolish chortling. When he was two or three months old your antics could trigger a hearty belly laugh, and by his sixth month your interactions had risen to the level of mimicking each other's lip-rattling "raspberries." These were true, but often wordless, conversations. Each of you expected and received a response to the sounds you were making. These little chats were all very happy and positive, but they formed the foundation for more serious communications that were to come. Even when he was six months old your child could draw associations between what you said, how you said it, and what was going to happen next.

Now that your little baby has "grown legs" and has begun looking for adventure, he is not too young to understand that when you say a particular word (e.g., "No") with a certain tone in your voice, he can expect negative consequences. Your toddler or even your creeping nine-month-old is pretty smart. If chicks can learn to peck at colored lights in complex sequences and rats can run mazes without a false step, your one-year-old is more than capable of understanding what you mean when you say "No." He may have already demonstrated that he understands its meaning by saying "No" himself in response to most of your questions. The process of attaching words to consequences is *simple.* Unfortunately, applying it to your young child's behavior isn't always *easy,* and that is why I have written this book.

AND, IT CERTAINLY ISN'T TOO LATE. Although I have chosen to include the word "toddler" in the title of this book, *How to Say No . . .* contains strategies and principles that can be applied to children who are in preschool. Even if you have been inconsistent in how and when you have been saying "No" for years, there is still time to learn how to use the word effectively.

If your child is between ages one and five he is still very adaptable, and you will discover that success can come in just a matter of days, weeks at the longest. In fact I have spoken with scores of parents of four- and five-year-olds who have noticed significant improvement overnight after making one or two simple changes in their approach to behavior management. It is never too late to change your behavior and the way you talk with your child so that he knows that you mean what you say.

BUT IT GETS HARDER THE LONGER YOU WAIT. Compared to adolescence, the toddler years are far less complex. The situations in which you must say "No" to your two-year-old are pretty simple. "Don't run into the street!" "Don't play with the computer cords!" "Don't climb up on the kitchen counter!" The hazards in the life of a toddler are very real and the consequences of some of his misbehaviors every bit as serious as drinking and driving or unprotected sex, but when your child is two you don't have to compete with the powerful forces of peer pressure or the hormone-driven sexual curiosity of puberty.

For one thing, your toddler only weighs twenty-five or thirty pounds. You can pick him up and move him to a safer environment, and although it may leave you breathless, you can still outrun him. For the moment, you have some physical control over his behavior and the safety of his environment. By the time he reaches junior high, if not long before, you will need to rely more heavily on your ability to communicate with words alone. If you have a good track record of consistency that began when he was a toddler, your words will be much more effective when he is a teenager.

While it may sound far-fetched to speak about adolescent misbehavior and toddler mischievousness in the same breath, it's not. If your two-year-old has learned that he can trust what you say now and that he can believe your promises as well as your threats, you will have less trouble communicating with him when he gets older and the issues have become more complex. Don't get me wrong, I can't guarantee that if you read this book you won't have any trouble talking to your teenager. But I am sure that if you haven't mastered the ability to say "No" to your toddler in a way that he can understand, adolescence will be far more difficult than it needs to be . . . for both of you.

SAFETY IS THE BOTTOM LINE. While none of us wants to be thought of as the parent of a "spoiled brat," it is your child's safety and not his reputation that is the most compelling reason to learn to say "No" to your toddler *now*. Of course he might learn that oven doors can burn his hands and electric cords can shock him through a process of trial and error, but I'm sure you would prefer that your child learn about these dangers and arrive at adulthood without the scars of his failed experiments.

Getting ORGANIZED

As you explore the chapter headings, you may notice that the parts of behavior management parents find the most difficult, such as administering consequences, are presented last. The rationale for this arrangement goes beyond mere procrastination. Many misbehaviors can be tempered, avoided, or completely eliminated by careful attention to their causes and the situations in which they erupt. This means that by making some rather simple and easily achieved changes in your day-to-day family routines you may never need to administer the more dramatic consequences that most parents find so challenging.

This is why we will start with a bit of introspection about why "No" is such a difficult word to say. Then you and I will walk around your child's environment searching for the causes of her misbehaviors. At the same time we will be asking ourselves what role you may be playing in their occurrence. As a first step in preventing them we will prioritize her misbehaviors to make the job easier.

Next I will give you a blueprint from which you can build a discipline boundary that will be appropriate for your child's developmental stage and temperament. This limit-setting process will continue throughout her childhood, and like your own home it will need to be remodeled from time to time to meet the changing needs of your family.

With these limits in place we will look at the menu of responses at your disposal. I will describe why, over the course of thirty years of watching children and their parents, *time-out* has emerged as the safest and most effective consequence. We will explore the reasons that it may not have worked for you in the past and then give it another try with a few important changes.

The rest of the book is the icing on the cake. We will look at topics like the fine points of making threats, managing misbehaviors when you aren't at home, and what to do when you have issued a threat you couldn't keep. The last chapter contains a list of scenarios in which you will see how the basic principles of behavior management we have discussed can be applied to real-life toddler misbehaviors.

BOYS WILL BE BOYS, BUT . . . It is clear to those of us who are surrounded by children day in and day out that little boys usually present more disciplinary challenges than little girls. Clinical researchers have found that boys in general are more noncompliant. Unfortunately, these observations are of no consolation to the parents of a three-year-old girl who doesn't seem to understand when they tell her "No."

You will notice that in some sections of the book I refer to the child as "he" and others as "she." For the most part this gender assignment was random. However, when discussing a behavior that is more typical of a gender, I chose the more appropriate pronoun.

CHAPTER

2

Why a Simple
NO
Doesn't Work

Why It's Hard to Say NO

IT JUST IS. Most of us don't like confrontations and would rather avoid them at almost any cost. Maybe that's why we are so quick to hire lawyers to settle our disagreements. Faced with an argument, our blood pressure goes up and our palms begin to sweat. Confrontations simply aren't fun.

Everyone enjoys watching other people enjoying themselves, and if the happy person is our own child the pleasure is more than doubled. But we have seen enough to understand that having a good time can be dangerous. For example, we remember how much fun it was to use our bed as a trampoline, but we know that if our toddler keeps bouncing, sooner or later he's going to land head-first on the floor. We also realize that telling him to stop will trigger a tantrum, or at least a pout that could last for fifteen or twenty minutes, or that we might need to wrestle him to the floor before he will stop.

Watching someone weep makes us uncomfortable, and we naturally avoid doing things that might make our child cry. Tantrums can be even more difficult to ignore, particularly if they occur in public, although that is the strategy that most behavior specialists suggest. It's not surprising that most of us will bend the rules and forget our threats to avoid a tearful, foot-stomping, head-banging meltdown.

> There is no getting around it. Saying "No" runs counter to our natural instincts, but our children's survival depends on our ability to do it.

We all want our children to be safe, but we also want them to be happy. Herein lies the dilemma.

YOU DON'T HAVE A RATIONAL PLAN OF SAFE CONSEQUENCES. You may find it difficult to say "No" because you aren't sure what to do when your child ignores your warnings. If you haven't found a consequence that is both safe and effective, it doesn't make sense to confront your child's misbehavior. For example, the last time your toddler took off toward the street you may have tapped him on the bottom with the flat of your hand. He probably laughed it off, and you felt foolish. Are you prepared to hit him harder the next time to make him understand? I bet you won't. On the other hand, if you had struck him so hard that it raised a red welt and he cried, I'm sure you'd think twice before you spanked him again.

You have also been challenged by less dangerous behaviors such as dropping toys into the toilet or the dog's feeding bowl. These are merely annoying infractions of the rules of civility, but you feel they demand some response.

Long ago you realized that yelling louder and repeating yourself a dozen times doesn't work. More recently you may have tried your toddler in a time-out chair that didn't work either, because he wouldn't stay put unless you stood behind him. The bottom line is that you don't have an "or else" to follow up your "No." The result is that you are much less likely to say "Stop" if you don't feel comfortable finishing the sentence with "or I'm going to . . ."

YOU DON'T WANT TO SOUND LIKE YOUR PARENTS. Your parents may have resorted to spanking and abusive language when you misbehaved. It was wasn't fun growing up under their system, and you don't want to run the risk of repeating their mistakes with your own toddler. You have promised yourself that you won't strike your child or run your house like a penal colony, but you haven't discovered a workable alternative. You know what you don't want to do, but for the moment you are left without a way of saying "No" that your toddler understands . . . and obeys.

YOU ARE TOO TIRED. Like most children your toddler's behavior degenerates as the day progresses and he becomes more fatigued. To compound the problem you are also getting tired and cranky by late afternoon. Without the stamina to confront your child's misbehaviors or follow through with the necessary consequences, you are simply too tired to say "No" effectively. This important fact of life is one that most behavioral specialists overlook in their advice to parents. As you read this book, I will continue to remind you that sleep, both yours and your child's, is critical to your parental success and satisfaction. Many chapters will contain practical tips that will help your family develop healthy sleep habits. When you are all well rested, there will be fewer confrontations and you will be better prepared to respond to them when they occur.

YOU FEEL GUILTY. Guilt is one of the most important issues that parents must grapple with as they try to shepherd their children toward adulthood. There are occasions when we all feel that we aren't giving our children enough time or attention, but for some of us who work outside the home, a cloud of guilt hangs over us all day long.

When you finally return home at the end of a long day at the office, the last thing you want to say is "No," even when you know the situation demands it. Guilt is one of the dark sides of being a parent, whether you stay at home or are a partner in a two-income family, but it is a fact of life in twenty-first-century North America that we must accept. Maybe if we talked about it more, and were more open about sharing our feelings, it would be easier to manage.

I can't claim to make parenting a guilt-free experience,

and I will continue to remind you that you must be honest about your own emotions if you are going to be successful. When I look back at my own experience as a parent it was I and not my three children who suffered most from my frequent absences. They have grown up to be fine adults and they tell me I have nothing to feel guilty about. But I still regret that I missed out on some wonderful opportunities.

The bottom line is that even though you wish you could apologize to your child for being away all day or sounding cranky, you must say "No" when your child's health and safety are at stake. Learning to say the word so that your child will understand is about communicating honestly. Don't give yourself one more thing to feel guilty about by talking to your child in parental double-talk.

YOU WANT TO FEEL IN CONTROL. Successful parenting means that by the time he is an adult you will have given your child control over his own life. Many of the steps in the process will be difficult, particularly if like me you are a bit of a control freak. You may have taken the first step when you realized that you *can't* stop your child from throwing toys on the floor simply because you don't want them there. While you must accept the inevitability of your child's eventual independence, you can have some control over the pace at which it occurs.

YOU ARE DEPRESSED. You may have had periods of depression in high school or college, and now that you are faced with the stress of parenting a toddler, the dark cloud has returned. You may have had postpartum depression that has been slow to resolve. The blue moments you have diagnosed as sleep deprivation may actually be a combination of fatigue *and* depression.

Pediatricians and child psychologists have observed that depressed parents have more trouble managing their children's behavior. It may be time to talk to your doctor about getting some help with your bouts of sadness.

"NO" Isn't Working

THE PROBLEM DIDN'T BEGIN YESTERDAY. Although it may feel like your problems with saying "No" began when your child began to crawl, you have been struggling to enforce limits since long before your toddler started to explore the dangers that lurk under kitchen cabinets and behind entertainment centers. The initial test of your ability to say "No" surfaced when you tried to influence when and where your baby was going to sleep and eat.

Newborns prefer to sleep near their mothers, where it's warm and a sweet snack is available just a few inches away. If you decided that you were going to share your bed with your newborn, you postponed this first opportunity to say "No." On the other hand, if like most parents you decided that your baby was going to sleep in her own crib, you were saying "No" to your baby. "No, you can't sleep where you want." If you also tried to put her on an arbitrary four-hour feeding schedule, you were saying,

"No, you can't eat anytime that you feel just a little hungry." It wasn't easy, was it? In fact I'll bet that your child protested and more often than not you gave in and brought her in bed with you or fed her well before the four hours were up. Like most parents, without help and encouragement from your family and your pediatrician you probably found it too difficult to say "No" to your two-month-old enough times to accomplish these two "unnatural" goals of independent sleep and scheduled feedings.

While you may be tempted to consider these initial attempts at saying "No" as failures, they aren't. You didn't do anything wrong. However, these first experiences with setting limits should have warned you that "taking candy from a baby" wasn't going to be as easy as some might have you believe. Or maybe you were successful. Bravo! That stick-to-it-iveness will serve you well over the next months and years.

YOU HAVE BEEN AFRAID TO SAY THE WORD. Have you been afraid that saying "No" too often or that setting too many limits will stifle your child's creativity? You don't want to run your home like a prison, and you want your child to feel free to express herself, explore her environment, and learn on her own by trial and error. It is true that your toddler must explore to learn, but you must set some limits to protect her from the dangers she encounters on her safaris into the jungle around her. The trick is learning how to draw boundaries that will keep her safe and still allow her room to create, learn, and explore. You will soon learn that it isn't as difficult as you have imagined.

While you may have been afraid to say "No" simply because you don't like confrontations, you also may have been afraid to say "No" because you didn't have a plan of what to do if your child didn't respond to your warning. You have heard that good parents shouldn't spank, and it wasn't an option you would have considered anyway. Redirecting your toddler to a safer activity worked for a short time, but your child's ability to find more mischief was far greater than your ability to find new and less dangerous activities. You have tried time-out, but your child won't stay in the time-out chair. Left without a humane or effective consequence, you are afraid to say "No" because you can't think of an "or else." Or you just say "No" again and again without much effect.

YOU HAVE BEEN TALKING TOO MUCH. You may have been treating your toddler as though she were an adult by trying to explain to her why her behaviors are dangerous or annoying. While it is important to discuss things with your child, most of the discipline issues you have been struggling with simply can't be negotiated. By attempting to reason with your toddler instead of creating and administering appropriate consequences,

> You can't simply talk your child into behaving properly, but there are ways to incorporate discussion into a successful behavior management plan.

your "No" has become just another word in a dialogue that your child knows she can drag out until you give in.

YOUR EXPECTATIONS HAVE BEEN UNREALISTIC. Few of us have taken a course in developmental psychology before we decided to have a child. In this state of ignorant bliss we may harbor unrealistic expectations for our toddler's behavior. We may assume that any two-year-old can sit quietly in a church pew for more than ten minutes. We may assume that most three-year-olds can learn to share.

Your child has come into the world with her own combination of temperament and attention span. Just because your two-year-old nephew will play quietly with a toy bulldozer for twenty minutes doesn't mean that you can expect your two-and-a-half-year-old to do the same. If you have been trying to set limits that are inappropriate for your child's personality and developmental stage, you have been saying "No" so often that the word has lost its meaning, and you must be exhausted.

An important part of learning how to say "No" to your toddler is discovering how to set limits that will keep her safe *and* that you can expect her to respect. These boundaries may be different from those your next-door neighbors have instituted for their toddler. The boundaries must also be flexible so that they can be adjusted as your child matures. In the next chapter I will tell you how this can be done.

YOU'VE BEEN SAYING "NO" WHEN YOU SHOULD HAVE BEEN SAYING, "IT'S BEDTIME!" You may have been trying to discipline a toddler whose primary problem is sleep deprivation. An overtired child is more likely to misbehave, and she is also less likely to respond to your attempts to correct her behavior. The solution to your discipline problems may simply be creating an appropriate sleep schedule for your toddler. Once she is well rested, your "No!" will be much more effective. (In Chapter 3, I will tell you how to correct her sleep problems).

YOUR "NO'S" HAVEN'T BEEN FOLLOWED BY APPROPRIATE OR EFFECTIVE CONSEQUENCES. By far the most likely reason that your toddler isn't heeding your warnings is that they have seldom been followed by meaningful consequences. There is the old saying that "talk is cheap." Of course it is very important to talk with your child. Words can be powerful, and when poorly chosen they can hurt feelings and destroy egos. However, if you have been saying "No" without an "or else," or without administering a threatened consequence, you have worn out the word by misusing it (and probably several others). "No" has become devalued to the point that it is worthless in your struggle to correct your child's behavior.

Listen to yourself for just an hour, and see how many times you say "No" or "Don't" or "Stop that" without mentioning a consequence. If you do make a threat, how often do you follow through? It doesn't take very many of these false alarms before your child will begin to ignore them.

Where SHALL WE START?
(Remember, Rome Wasn't Built in a Day)

Let's start by agreeing on what it means to be a "well-behaved" toddler. Because each child reaches her first birthday with her own particular level of curiosity and tolerance for quiet play, it may be unfair to label the explorations of your active and inquisitive toddler as "bad" behavior. It may be risky or annoying, but what's "bad" about the behavior may be when and where it is occurring. For example, squirming in a church pew isn't any different from changing positions on a couch twenty-five times during a thirty-minute TV program. It's really just a matter of being in the wrong place at the wrong time.

> A well-behaved child is one who, when placed in appropriate situations, responds positively to her parents' requests.

On the other hand, we could define "well-behaved" in terms of how a child responds to the requests of her parents or other adults. For example, when you tell your toddler to stop pulling books off of a shelf, does she obey?

While level of obedience may be a better way to define "good" behavior, the best description of a "well-behaved child" is one that also acknowledges her parents' role in choosing and modifying her environment.

DETAILS, DETAILS . . . Before we begin solving your problem, we must define it. Of course we know that the big problem is that your toddler doesn't seem to understand that when you say "No," you mean "Stop that misbehavior, now!" That's why you picked up this book. But the question is too broad. While there is some general advice I can offer every parent about managing his or her child's behavior, if we really want to fix your problem we need to get right down to the nuts and bolts and start dealing with specifics. By dissecting the causes for your child's misbehaviors, we will improve our chances of finding the solutions that will work *and* continue to work, week after week, month after month.

Many parents who come to my office seeking help with their toddler's misbehaviors feel overwhelmed. Lulled into complacency by their baby's first blissful and unadventurous year, they suddenly find their lives turned upside down by a deluge of toddler exploration and testing. Like you, they may not know where to start. Every behavior seems to be a challenge. When she's in her high chair she's throwing food. When she's out in the yard she's running for the street. When she is in the house, nothing less than three feet off the floor is safe, and yesterday she learned that she can use a kitchen chair as a ladder. Bedtimes are a struggle and nap times are hit or miss. Half the trips to the grocery store end in meltdowns or tantrums.

The first step toward parental sanity is backward to take a long look at the whole picture. In this section we will examine your child's misbehaviors and the situations in which they occur. We will look first for causes that we can remedy quickly and easily, and then we will prioritize so that we will get the most benefit for our efforts. You will be surprised how quickly many things improve before we even begin talking about setting limits and administering consequences.

First, let's cut the problem into bite-sized pieces.

WHICH BEHAVIORS ARE BOTHERING YOU THE MOST? I suggest that you get a pencil and paper and *make a list*. Try to be as specific as you can. "She's cranky all the time" or "She never does what I ask her to do" are too general. I trust that after you have finished this book and applied the strategies it describes, these broad complaints will evaporate, but for the moment we want to get down to the nitty gritty.

"She throws food when she is in her high chair." "It takes us until nine o'clock to get her to sleep." "She keeps punching buttons on the CD player." "She pitches a fit in the grocery store if I don't put everything she wants into the cart." These are the kinds of specific complaints that we will need to start the process. Eventually, we will want

> Arguing with your partner about how to manage your toddler's misbehaviors may be a bigger problem than the behaviors themselves.

even more information about each of these situations, but for the moment this level of detail is sufficient.

Things may seem so out of control that once you start

writing you could easily fill both sides of an eight-and-a-half-by-eleven sheet of paper, but try to keep your list to ten behaviors or less. This will be our first crude pass at prioritization. A list that's too long will leave both of us feeling overwhelmed.

Even though only one of you may think that your child's behavior is a problem, each parent should make his or her own list. One of the most difficult aspects of parenting is that it is a shared task. In Chapter 4 ("Putting Your Plan to Work") we will discover how to reconcile your different perspectives, but for now the process of creating your separate lists can help us determine realistic priorities.

If you are going to be successful, you both must be on the same page, and that is one of the reasons I decided to write this book. To get the ball rolling, let's start by committing your observations to paper.

DON'T INCLUDE BAD MANNERS AND IMPOLITE BEHAVIOR ON YOUR LIST. This is a good place for us to pause briefly and agree on what we *can't* accomplish with discipline. As I mentioned earlier in the introduction and will remind you again later in this chapter, your first priority should be your child's safety. Her health and survival will be our primary concerns as we create limits and choose appropriate consequences. A secondary motive is protecting the environment from her attempts to destroy it. However, discipline is not the way to teach your toddler good manners.

I'm sure you have met children who seem painfully polite. Their "yes, ma'ams," "yes, sirs," and "thank yous" have a hollow, insincere ring to them. It makes you wonder what their parents have done to engender these theatrical performances. Whenever I meet one of these overly well-mannered little automatons, I think it must not be much fun living at home with her parents.

Don't get me wrong. I think that good manners are extremely important, but minding her p's and q's can wait. *After* we have gotten your toddler's unsafe behaviors under control we will discuss some strategies for discouraging the typical, but unpleasant, behaviors such as spitting unwanted food back onto her plate.

> *P*olite behavior is something that is best learned by example and not by making threats and administering consequences.

If your child observes you treating other people discourteously and disrespectfully, the odds are that she will grow up to do the same. I can't guarantee that if you are polite and well mannered your child will be as well, but it's your best shot. It never hurts to remind your toddler to say "please" and "thank you," and from time to time an *older* child may need to be threatened with consequences to remind her of the importance of polite behavior. But your child is still a toddler. For the moment let's focus our attention on the more serious issues that are typical of her age group and let our examples teach her good manners.

WHEN DO THE PROBLEM BEHAVIORS OCCUR? Most misbehaving children are overtired. Tantrums occur more frequently when children are sleep deprived. Researchers have discovered that children who are short on sleep are more likely to have accidents that require emergency-room treatment. Neurologists have observed that hyper-activity, distractibility, and a decreased attention span, symptoms we usually associate with attention deficit disorders (ADD and ADHD), can appear in children who simply aren't getting enough sleep.

This association between sleep and childhood behavior has become so obvious over my thirty years in pediatric practice that it prompted me to write a book devoted to the subject *(Is My Child Overtired?* Simon and Schuster, 2000). Simply helping your child develop healthy sleep habits will eliminate many of the confrontations in which you've been saying "No" unsuccessfully. As you read on you will learn how to weave fatigue prevention into your broader behavior management plan.

Let's go back to your list of misbehaviors and look at when one is most likely to occur. I suspect you will discover that many of the behaviors cluster in the late afternoon and late morning because these are the times when your child is getting tired. If your child is cranky and disagreeable first thing in the morning, particularly if you have had to wake her to get off to daycare, this is another sign that some of her orneriness is the result of being overtired. When it is time to talk about priorities and solutions, we will come back to this issue of sleep deprivation. For the moment, file these observations about the timing of your toddler's misbehaviors in the back of your mind, and let's continue our search for clues.

WHERE DO THE BEHAVIORS OCCUR? Do you feel that you are knocking heads with your toddler from the time she gets up in the morning until the time she goes to bed, but when you complain to your daycare providers they sound surprised. According to them, your child is very compliant and seldom tests the limits they set. Is this simply a matter of timing? It could be that the daycare providers see her when she is rested and by the time she gets home she is overtired. Or are the daycare providers' behavior management plans working better than yours?

On the other hand, you may not be having any trouble getting your toddler to understand what "No" means, but her daycare providers may report that she is aggressive. They may have warned you that if her behavior doesn't improve soon, you'll be looking for another daycare. It's possible you have become so accustomed to her bad behaviors that you have begun to accept them as normal.

It's more likely that something is amiss at daycare. The provider-to-child ratio may have slipped. The addition of a new child to the mix may have displaced your child from her comfort zone. We will talk about managing misbehavior at daycare in detail in Chapters 3, 4, and 5, but for now we are just gathering evidence to help us formulate a plan.

Is your toddler more likely to misbehave when she is at Grandma's house or at the grocery store or at play group? Again, the answer may be that she goes to those places at a time of day when she is too tired to behave and the solution is simply to change her schedule so that she arrives at these places well rested. However, there may be something about the atmosphere at those locations that is contributing to the problem. Are there too many people? Is it too noisy or warm? Is one of her playmates a bully? As you read on you may discover the explanation, but for the moment the answer may be to avoid those places where her behavior is a problem.

WHEN DID THE BEHAVIORS BEGIN? The answer is probably that they gradually began to appear as your baby evolved from an infant who traveled by rolling into a toddler with legs that could run and words she could craft into questions. With her newly acquired skills comes a natural inclination to test limits. As the parent of a toddler you must be prepared to deal with an array of new behaviors; not all of them will be cute or a reason for you to brag.

However, some behavioral eruptions may be the result of changes in her environment. For example, did her tantrums become more frequent when you or your partner began a different work schedule? Although your total time away from home may not have changed, the timing of your absences may not fit your toddler's emotional needs. Don't assume that her initial reaction will be positive just because you are at home more.

Did the behaviors get worse after she started daycare or you changed baby-sitters? Have there been any births, deaths (don't forget pets), divorces, or illnesses in the extended family? Children, particularly toddlers, are very sensitive to unspoken tension. Have you had visitors? Strangers in the house, even invited guests, can be very unsettling. The association between some of these environmental changes and her behavior may not make much sense to you or me. That's just one of the things that makes dealing with toddlers so "interesting."

WHO HAS THE BIGGEST PROBLEM GETTING YOUR TODDLER TO UNDERSTAND "NO"? It may be you because you are at home all day and have had to deal with so many misbehaviors that your threats have lost their meaning. When you hear yourself saying, "No, don't go in there. No, put that down! Not now, it's time for your nap" time after time, eventually you wonder if it is worth it. If you haven't been able to come up with appropriate or meaningful consequences, then your child may have stopped listening. Your partner, on the other hand, may arrive on the scene, maybe not well rested, but at least with a fresh perspective, a different tone of voice and a threshold for misbehavior that is two rungs higher than yours. Suddenly your toddler begins responding to the same threats that she was ignoring when you made them a half an hour earlier. It's frustrating and makes you look foolish, but it happens all the time.

On the other hand, you may be the one who arrives home so exhausted from a long day at the office that you wonder if you will find the energy to play with your toddler, but of course you do. However, by the time it comes to saying "No, you can't have goldfish crackers for dinner tonight" for the third time, you've run out of steam and give in. Caving in will earn you the label as the weak link in the family. You can expect to be the "go-to" guy or girl whenever your toddler wants something she knows is on the forbidden list.

It is tempting to view these differences in terms of gender. Most men come to a confrontation with a lower, more forceful voice that may convey an unspoken threat. Even though we may be totally unprepared to carry out our threats, men do often create a more intimidating first impression. Bigger isn't always better or more consistent, but your toddler may not understand that in the beginning. Eventually she'll notice if her father doesn't follow up on his threats either. Until then she will be hesitant to call his bluff. Of course we all know women whose voice and body language command respect from toddlers and truck drivers alike. My mother was one of them.

Regardless of gender, there are bound to be differences in parenting style between you and your partner. You may be the one who draws stricter limits, and you may also be the one who finds it easier to carry through with consequences. Or it may be your partner who is the more natural disciplinarian. For the moment let's accept those differences as a given and resist the temptation to view them in qualitative terms. It may be *easier* for your partner to say "No," but that doesn't make him or her a *better* parent.

In the long run our goal is a safe, rational, and effective discipline program that both of you can agree on and use to help your child grow up healthy and happy. Finger-pointing won't help us achieve that goal. In Chapter 4 we will talk about how to resolve these differences in style.

HOW OFTEN DOES THE BEHAVIOR OCCUR? The answer to this question will help you prioritize later on. If your toddler likes to undress herself and run around the house naked, we can agree that if she only does it once every few weeks, it doesn't qualify as a problem behavior that demands immediate attention. However, if she strips down every time you turn your back, that is a misbehavior worthy of your prompt response, even though it should be lower on your list than such safety-related behaviors as running into the street or climbing up onto the kitchen counter.

You have completed your list. For the moment, let's set it aside and look further into the reasons that your child is misbehaving. We will come back to it later when it is time to prioritize and set limits.

Why Is Your Child
MISBEHAVING?

LET'S LOOK UNDER ALL THE ROCKS. You have finished an inventory of your child's misbehaviors and considered when, where, with whom, and how often they occur. These observations have given us a few hints about *why* your child is misbehaving. Now it's time to dig deeper.

Other books about toddler behavior focus too narrowly on the child and his misbehaviors. The authors may have been afraid of being "judgmental" if they pried too deeply into the parental role in toddler misbehaviors. Unfortunately, by failing to ask what could be difficult questions they may not discover the answers to your family's discipline problems.

Your child is not being raised in a vacuum. He has two parents, both of whom may have jobs outside the home and both of whom must face a wide array of other stressors on a daily basis. We are not going to ignore this fact in our investigation, and I won't be afraid to suggest changes in how you organize your life and prioritize your time if I know they will make parenting go more smoothly for you. Please don't interpret my observations and suggestions as "judgmental." Just because I am asking you to examine your role in your child's misbehaviors doesn't mean that I believe you are necessarily one of the major contributors. Nor does it mean that I think you or any other parent seeking help in how to say "No" is a bad parent.

There are other people and situations that we may want to include in our investigation. If your child goes to a daycare, he must interact with more adults and a classroom full of other toddlers. He may also have a sibling with whom he must share space and parental attention. He may have grandparents who share in his care. All of these people and their environments can affect his behavior. Once you understand what makes your toddler tick (and misbehave), you can make changes in his surroundings that will make limit setting more rational and the administration of consequences a less frequent event.

THE MYTH OF THE TYPICAL TODDLER. One of the nice things about working with young children is that their needs are simple and their responses far less complex than those of older children and adolescents. However, don't fall into the trap of interpreting that lack of complexity as uniformity. Your toddler is as different from his daycare mates as you and your partner are from each other. Although most two-year-old boys are hell-bent for adventure, your son may be shy and easily deterred by your simply raising your voice. He may have tantrums when he is overtired while your neighbor's toddler curls up quietly on the couch and falls asleep. You may need to tell your three-year-old something seven times before he understands, while your niece appears to grasp the concept on the first attempt. Each child is a unique blend of strengths and vulnerabilities. Any parent who has raised more than one child will tell you that there is no such thing as a typical two-year-old.

When it is time to talk about setting limits, we will revisit this issue of uniqueness. For the moment let's assume that the only similarity between toddlers is their age.

CURIOSITY. Although there are times when your toddler will intentionally act out to get your attention, most of his misbehaviors are a consequence of the compulsion to explore. For nearly a year he was trapped in a body that wouldn't take him anywhere. When he became a capable crawler his world expanded to include a buffet of objects and opportunities to tempt his appetite for adventure. Your curious toddler wants to touch, feel, taste, and tinker.

Unfortunately, his environment isn't always child-friendly.

He has entered one of the steep places on the learning curve that we call life, but he prefers to experiment himself rather than take your word for it. Obviously, you can't allow him to discover for himself that hot curling irons burn and that playing in the street can be deadly. You must set limits to keep him safe, and you must expect that he will challenge those rules because he doesn't understand their importance.

> Your toddler is going to misbehave because he is curious and doesn't always anticipate the consequences of his explorations.

IS HE OVERTIRED? If your child wanders around with his pacifier (or thumb) in his mouth, or must have his blanket or special stuffed toy with him at all times, he isn't getting enough sleep. If he falls asleep any time he is in a moving car for more than ten minutes, your toddler is sleep deprived. If he must be awakened in the morning or from naps, he isn't being allowed to repay his accumulating sleep debt. If your child wakes at night with leg pains or has frequent night terrors he is overtired. If your two-year-old is getting less than thirteen hours of sleep (combination night sleep and naps) he isn't getting enough sleep. If he is three his requirement is at least twelve hours.

Because I have observed that at any one time more than three quarters of the patients in my practice aren't getting enough sleep, I am sure that you have noticed at least one of these symptoms of sleep deprivation in your own child. When it is time to prioritize our discipline strategies we will return to this important issue.

IS YOUR TODDLER GETTING ENOUGH "QUALITY TIME" WITH YOU? While sleep deprivation and his natural curiosity are the most likely causes of your toddler's misbehavior, let's not underestimate the importance of your time and attention. Although when he is a teenager his primary motivation will seem to be peer pressure, your child will always care what you think about him. He wants you to approve of his behavior, but if that isn't going to happen, your negative attention will do.

Young children are concrete thinkers and don't have much capacity for delayed gratification. This means that you must be present to give your toddler the attention he craves. You can't mail it in and a phone call doesn't do the job. Even if you are in the same room your child can tell when your mind is somewhere else.

This fact of life presents a problem for those of us with jobs, particularly if we work outside the home. A few children can learn to postpone their needs until we have time for them, but every child has his limit. When we aren't there to play or comfort or simply just acknowledge they exist, misbehaviors erupt. Your toddler may be angry or sad that you aren't paying attention to him. In either case the behavior could be a violent tantrum, an obstinate withdrawal, or a daredevil performance.

In the last few years the unfortunate term "quality

time" has crept into our language. It's popularity reflects the awareness by many parents that they aren't giving their children enough attention. They hope that improving the quality of the time they spend with their children will compensate for its lack of quantity.

There are two problems with this rationalization. First, parental attention is like food. If you are starving, one perfect Macintosh apple won't satisfy your hunger as well as three bruised ones. In other words, if your child needs or wants attention, a dose of quality time that is too small won't solve the problem.

The second problem is that it is usually parents and not their children who define quality time. For example, most small children are early risers and fast starters; by late afternoon the best part of their day is behind them. At five o'clock many toddlers are too tired to even eat much of a dinner. If you arrive home at 6:30 expecting to spend some "quality time" with your two-year-old, you may have missed your opportunity to have some quality time, at least from the toddler's perspective. Your child may be too tired and cranky to play, even though you may be one of his favorite playmates. On the other hand, he may be stimulated into an ill-timed burst of energy that will delay his bedtime past a healthy hour.

Unfortunately, his definition doesn't always fit into

> It is your child who should define quality time.

your schedule. If you have noticed a recent increase in your child's misbehaviors, look at how you have allotted your time. Are you away from home more? Are you arriving home later? When you are at home are you distracted by phone calls or visitors when you could be playing with your child? Quality time doesn't always mean that the two of you must be interacting. He may be content that you are within sight while he plays with his trucks.

Rearranging schedules isn't easy, but it may be an important part of the solution to your toddler's misbehaviors. If his tantrums are a request for more parental attention, you must find him some more quality time, but remember he's the one who defines the quality.

COULD YOUR MISBEHAVING TODDLER BE SICK? Imagine how bad you would feel if, after sending your toddler to his room a half a dozen times in one morning, he vomits his lunch, and you discover that he has a temperature of 102°F. This may have already happened to you. Don't be surprised if it happens again.

Sometimes illnesses will creep up on you with little or no warning. Try to resist your natural inclination to feel guilty in these situations. All of us have had days when we tried to discipline our children for behavior that in retrospect was an early symptom of a sickness.

There is a lesson to be learned from these unfortunate scenarios. If your toddler is cranky day after day for as much as a week or more and you are sure that he is getting enough sleep, it is time to take him to the pediatrician. You may have overlooked a chronic, low-grade illness that is sapping his strength and making him uncomfortable. Recall how you felt and behaved the last time you were sick.

Not every infection is accompanied by a fever high enough for you to notice. Urinary tract infections, a problem that is more common in girls, may not be associated with any of the symptoms that you would expect in older children, such as a burning feeling with urination or frequent voiding. In fact crankiness and misbehavior may be the only obvious symptoms.

If your child has chronic ear or sinus infections he may not complain of pain and may not have a fever. Part of the problem is that your toddler lacks the vocabulary to adequately describe what hurts and how he feels. Even those of us who have been speaking for years often can't find the words to describe that general malaise that we feel when we know we are sick but aren't exactly sure what is bothering us.

When you take your toddler to the pediatrician be careful to explain the situation completely. Tell him or her that your child's behavior has been a problem and that before you begin setting limits and making threats, you would like to be sure that your child is healthy. After examining your child the pediatrician will probably be able to reassure you that he is fine and that you can expect him to understand age-appropriate boundaries and respond to a strategy that includes rational consequences.

ARE YOU DEPRESSED? I asked you this question when we were examining why saying "No" is so difficult. It comes up again because I have observed that depressed parents are more likely to complain about their children's behavior. I have been tempted to attribute this observation to the fact that when we are depressed we focus on the negative. In this case the depressed parent may see his or her child's misbehaviors as dominating, when in reality he is well behaved most of the time. Some children simply seem to misbehave more when one of their parents is depressed.

If you have a past history of depression or you find it difficult to have any cheerful or positive thoughts, talk to your doctor about your feelings. Your mental state may or may not be contributing to your child's behavior problems, but it certainly is going to make it hard for you to participate in their solution.

IS YOUR MARRIAGE SHAKY? Some scientists suspect that animals have the ability to sense subterranean tremors long before we humans feel the earthquake. Toddlers have a similar ability to detect marital unrest before it is obvious to adults.

Your child may or may not have heard you argue, but he can feel the negative vibrations. Some toddlers will become clingy and suffer a relapse of stranger-anxiety when they sense the family ship is rocking. Others will react with tantrums or an outburst of risky behaviors.

Even if you don't think that your toddler's misbehavior is the result of your marital troubles, now is the time to get some help. Your pediatrician will probably know a family therapist who can help. If the issues are relatively minor, you can work them out before they cause deep scars.

CHAPTER
3

Using "No"
and Other Ways to
MANAGE
BEHAVIOR
Effectively

Redirection, Rhetoric, and
REWARDS

UP TO A POINT. You may have heard that the best way to manage your toddler's bad behavior is to redirect him to a preferred behavior, explain to him why his original choice was a poor one, and then reward him for his good behavior. It is hard to find fault with these recommendations because they seem to make good sense. In fact they work more often than they fail. The problem is that like most parents you have probably encountered many situations in which the basic three Rs haven't kept a young child's misbehaviors in check.

If you have a placid, compliant, and unadventurous toddler (and, yes, they do exist), then redirection, discussion, and positive reinforcement do work. However, if your child's behaviors were that easy to manage, you probably wouldn't have picked up this book. Although these strategies may not have always done the trick for you, don't discard them. They still deserve a place in your discipline plan. Let's take a few moments to examine their strengths and shortcomings.

REDIRECTION—HOW LONG CAN YOU STAY ONE STEP AHEAD? Most behavioral specialists recommend that your first step in managing your toddler's behavior is to redirect him to a more acceptable and less dangerous activity. For example, if your child begins to tug on the tangle of wires behind your computer, you are instructed to pick him up, move him to another part of the room, and sit him on the floor with one of his favorite trucks.

If he abandons the trucks after a few minutes and returns to play in the wire jungle, the redirection strategy says that you pick him up again and re-seat him with his trucks. If they fail to hold his interest, find another distraction, such as his set of giant blocks. When your imagination and his supply of toys has been exhausted, the next step should be out the door to the backyard or playground. A change in scene may finally do the trick.

If you have tried re-direction you know that some days it works and your child decides his toys are more interesting than the computer wires. And some days it doesn't. If the lure of the forbidden jungle is too strong, you are in for a battle of determination. If you are too tired or are trying to send an e-mail to a client, you may not have the time or stamina to continue the search for a distraction that will hold your toddler's interest long enough so that he forgets about the wires. If you live in a small apartment or it is raining, you don't have the options of changing the scene.

The bottom line is that re-direction is a labor-intensive strategy that doesn't always work. It's big advantage is that it is safe because it doesn't require a consequence such as spanking. With re-direction your goal is to find a toy or activity that makes your child happy, which avoids the unpleasantness of a confrontation. For this reason I suggest that you use redirection as your first option, even though there will be many times when your child's determination to misbehave is stronger than your emotional stamina and his imagination at finding trouble is greater than yours at creating distractions.

RHETORIC—TALK IS CHEAP. The centerpiece of some behavior management plans is discussion and negotiation. The advocates of this strategy encourage you to enter into a dialogue with your toddler to find out why he is misbehaving so that you can see the problem from his perspective. Next, the talk-oriented approach asks you to explain to your child why you think the behavior is dangerous or unpleasant. Finally, when you both understand each other's position you can arrive at a solution that makes you both happy.

You have probably heard parents try you use this strategy. "Aaron, you know that we have already talked about why poking Max with a stick could injure him. Can you think of something else you would like to do with the stick?" When the obvious first step would have been to take the stick away, the conversation may continue on exploring other, more acceptable uses for the stick or rehashing in gory detail what would happen to poor little Max if the stick were to puncture his lung.

Yes, it is important to talk to your child—to read to your child, to ask your child what he thinks about things and then listen to what he has to say. For example, you might be interested, even amused, to hear what prompted your toddler to feed the dog an entire bag of Halloween candy. But there are many situations in which a misbehavior must be stopped promptly and there is neither time for nor any benefit to be gained by discussing motives.

When your child is having a tantrum he isn't capable of rational discussion. If you ask him, "Why are you doing that?" The most likely answer is "I don't know." That is, if you get an answer at all. In fact your hysterical child may not be ready to answer any questions until he has had a good night's sleep. The time to discuss rules and their rationale is when everyone is well rested and there are no distractions.

In the morning your child may seem to have forgotten his misdeeds of the previous day, though a rehash of the ugly event may be the top item on your agenda. It never hurts to ask your toddler if he wants to talk about them, but don't push on with a one-sided discussion if your child isn't interested in talking about yesterday's misbehaviors.

As your toddler grows older he is more likely to understand your explanations. For example, a three-year-old can grasp the concept that he might fall when he is climbing on the bookcases. A one-and-a-half-year-old can't. Nonetheless, you will probably discover more about your toddler's motives by *listening* to what he says over the course of the day. If he wants to sit in your lap or bemoans the fact that you are going off to work, he may be craving your attention. If he uncharacteristically balks at going to preschool, he may have been bullied or he may be coming down with a virus.

Even if he is willing to talk about motives and consequences, remember that you are talking to a toddler who doesn't have a concept of death and may have only a fragmentary appreciation of injury gleaned from his own personal experiences. This means that when you tell Aaron that if he jabs Max with the stick he could poke his eye out or puncture his lung and he could stop breathing, it probably won't deter his behavior. Although he can grasp the concept of feeling sad, your child may not understand what it means to "hurt someone's feelings."

Of course your toddler understands some consequences. By the time he could sit, he knew that if he squeezed the rubber duck it quacked. But at two or three he doesn't really comprehend what it means to "get a shock" unless you have foolishly allowed him to experiment with a fork and a wall socket. There are just so many consequences that you can explain to him because he lacks the breadth of experiences with which to interpret your words. However, he can understand a consequence he has experienced such as spending time alone in his room.

In summary, it is important to ask your child what he

thinks and to listen to what he has to say, but as a strategy for dealing with repeated misbehaviors, talk by itself has serious limitations.

REWARDS—BRIBERY SELDOM WORKS. One of the cornerstones of behaviorist theory is that behavior can be molded by rewarding desired behaviors and administering unpleasant consequences for unwanted behaviors. This combination of positive and negative reinforcement works very well with laboratory animals and is at the heart of my approach to toddlers. However, *tangible* rewards don't seem to be as effective with children as they are with white rats. Nonetheless, many child psychologists recommend that parents develop a system of simple tokens such as stickers that can be accumulated on a chart or poker chips that can be redeemed for things the child likes, such as candy, toys, or trips to a fast-food restaurant. These reward systems have become very popular with some grade school teachers.

The arrangement can include a direct and immediate reward such as the direct: "If you put your jacket on without a fuss you will get a sticker." Or the indirect: "If you have a good morning without any tantrums, you can have a smiley face to put on your chart."

Both of these arrangements can work, but they have their limitations. The first is that most toddlers don't do well with delayed gratification. Asking your three-year-old to generate an entire morning of good behavior before she gets a reward is destined to fail more often than succeed.

Second, the behavior that is being rewarded must be discrete and easy to define so that your child can understand it. Being *good* all morning is a pretty vague concept for a toddler to grasp.

Another problem with reward systems is that they often become inflationary. How many trips to the fast-food restaurant will your child accept before she starts asking for a trip to Disney World? And then what? If you reward with food, your child may manipulate her behavior so well that she becomes obese. At the very least the practice will foster poor eating habits.

Rewards can result in a backlash. One scientific study I have read found that children who were rewarded for eating a food they didn't like responded positively in the beginning. However, after the reward was withdrawn they ate less of the unpreferred food than they had before the reward was offered.

Finally, the biggest downfall of reward systems is that they don't work over the long haul. I have witnessed some nice short-term success when reward systems have been instituted in managing discreet and minor misbehaviors such as leaving a messy bedroom. However, it is more likely these children will lose interest in the reward or their parents will find the system too cumbersome to maintain.

I don't want to discourage you from ever offering your toddler tangible rewards for good behavior, because this tactic, like redirection, is safe and can work, although not for very long. Tangible rewards can be used for the occasional minor misbehavior but should never become the centerpiece of your general behavior management plan. Ask yourself if you really want your child to grow up expecting a reward for every good behavior? As far as I can tell, the real world doesn't seem to work that way.

If you are going to use a tangible reward, define the behavior you want to reward carefully so that your child has a reasonable chance of achieving success. Keep the rewards small. Choose a preferred activity such as going to the playground instead of providing food or a handful of M&Ms and provide rewards often enough to maintain your child's interest in the program.

THE BEST REWARD. While tangible rewards for good behavior don't usually work, "positive reinforcement" should still play an important role in managing your child's behavior. Your toddler may tell you the thing she wants most is an action figure from the latest Disney movie, but your attention and approval are really what she values most. If your child is ever going to understand when you say "No," you must provide these two treasures in a timely fashion and in adequate amounts.

> If properly timed, your attention can serve as positive reinforcement for your toddler's good behavior and will be a far more powerful and long-lasting reward than stickers or a piece of candy.

While sleep deprivation is the most frequent, preventable cause of toddler misbehavior, attention-seeking is a close second. To avoid confrontations, you must see that your child gets enough sleep *and* attention.

Here is how it can work: Though there may be days that you feel your toddler has misbehaved every waking minute, the truth is that she is basically a good kid most of the time. Are you adequately rewarding her for her spells of good behavior? A bumper sticker that was popular in the eighties read, "Have you hugged your kid today?" It should have read, "Have you hugged your child *enough* today?"

Nonverbal, tactile evidence of approval, whether it is a hug, a pat on the head, a gentle squeeze of an arm, or a brief sit on your lap, sends a powerful message to your child that she's okay, you're okay, and her place in your family and the world is secure. These gestures may only take a few seconds, a few minutes at the most, but they reward your toddler for being who she is—a good kid. Of course she does misbehave from time to time and you must steer her back in the right direction. But every little hug or squeeze is an unspoken reminder that when she is behaving well, good things happen. These demonstrations of affection can be so brief and seemingly inconsequential that you don't have to interrupt your child's activity to employ them. It can be as simple as a tap on the head as you walk by her when she is sitting on the floor or a fifteen-minute cuddle in your lap.

Many years ago I read an article in which a psychologist described his experiences with young children who masturbated excessively. While I don't regard masturbation as a misbehavior, these children were definitely over-doing it. This scientist discovered that when parents did nothing more than touch or handle their children more often, the frequency of masturbation decreased significantly. (I discuss this topic in more detail in Chapter 4.)

You may say to yourself, this won't work on my child because she hates to be touched and the only time she sits in my lap is when she is sick. Yes, there are toddlers who instinctively recoil when they are touched. Some psychologists describe them as being "tactile defensive." However, even these children who don't like to cuddle will respond positively to brief, gentle, physical contact. Don't force your child to cuddle or sit in your lap. There are more than enough opportunities for brief, positive touching that won't require her cooperation.

You can embellish your physical displays of affection and approval with words, but they may not be necessary. Praise needn't be long and flowery, and it must be heartfelt. Little ears can hear the hollow ring of insincerity.

Hugging, cuddling, and touching should appear unconditional. Don't tell your child that "if" she is good you will hug her more. The point is that *when* she is good you give her more tactile attention, but you don't need to share this fact with her. It will become obvious to her in a subconscious and gentle way. Your actions will be speaking for you. Tactile attention is a reward that won't escalate beyond reasonable limits, and it has a lasting effect that tangible rewards lack.

Every squeeze and pat on the head helps avoid attention-seeking behavior, and they are investments that will pay dividends when it's time to choose a consequence for the inevitable misbehaviors. You will read that one of the reasons well-administered time-out is such a powerful consequence is that it temporarily separates your child from her source of attention and approval—you. The more attention you have been able to give your child when she is good, the more effective time-out will be when you remove it by sending her to her room. In other words, you can't take something away that your child doesn't already have.

> *P*arental praise is an important building block in a child's ego development. However, "overpraising" can foster an inflated self-image that is unlikely to survive when your toddler ventures into the "real world."

Ignorance . . .
NOT ALWAYS BLISSFUL
(If You Didn't See It, It Didn't Happen)

When you ask some behavioral specialists for advice the first question they will ask is, "Have you tried ignoring the behavior?" They know that many toddler misbehaviors are requests for attention and will continue as long as the child feels she is being watched.

You already know how difficult it is to ignore your child's misbehavior. She is just a few years old and for her own safety she must be watched almost every waking minute. How can you watch your toddler and ignore her at the same time? The answer is good acting. You may hear and see everything that is going on, but if you don't comment on the negative behavior, it doesn't exist. It is similar to that old brainteaser, "If a tree falls in the forest and there is no one there to hear it, does it make a sound?"

For example, if your toddler begins whining for a snack forty-five minutes before dinner, it is okay to answer "No, it will ruin your dinner" *once,* for educational purposes. But if you respond to the second whine, even if it is by snarling, "I've already told you no!" your child will continue the "conversation" by whining as long as you continue to reply.

I often hear parents tell their whining toddler to "use your words." Unfortunately, most children (young or old) aren't whining because they have forgotten the correct words. They have simply learned that whining is a more effective method of getting what they want.

If you suddenly become mute and continue fixing dinner as though you were alone in the kitchen, your child will eventually stop whining because she isn't receiving a response/reward. It may be an unpleasant ten or fifteen minutes, but the whining will stop. Your silence is an important investment that will pay dividends the next time your child starts whining. If she receives no feedback when she whines, your toddler will have to choose another tactic or, hopefully, wait patiently until dinner.

Silence alone may not be enough to make ignoring an effective deterrent. You must also be careful to avoid meeting your child's eyes. A glare is a wordless comment to which your toddler will reply by whining or misbehaving. Even if you bite your tongue and don't look directly at your child, your body language may reinforce his misbehavior. Toddlers can read and understand the subtleties of your tense posture and the angry slam of a cupboard door. A slip of the tongue or brief eye contact can undo your efforts.

To the observer the scenario is bizarre. The players are just a few feet apart. The child is screaming at the top of her lungs, but the adult, who seems to have all of her senses, appears unaware of the shrieking. She responds to the kitchen timer and answers the phone but doesn't seem to hear the child. She steps around her as though she were just another one of the stools at the breakfast counter. Ignoring is a charade, but one that works.

> Successful ignoring means behaving as though you are totally unaware that your child is misbehaving.

Ignoring harmless but annoying misbehaviors requires great patience and stamina, two things that many of us find in short supply at the end of the day. If you are going to try it, please don't skip the next chapter and miss what I have to say about the importance of sleep and how to become and remain a well-rested parent.

When a harmless behavior becomes dangerous or

when you can't keep up the act any longer, it's time to speak. Ignoring is an excellent behavior management strategy, but it has its limits. Sooner or later you will have to resort to threats and consequences.

What Works:
TRUTH AND CONSEQUENCES

If redirection, rhetoric, and rewards don't always work, and ignoring is difficult and impractical when safety is an issue, then how are you going to manage your toddler's behavior? The answer is: *Truth* and *Consequences*.

"Always tell your child the truth" sounds like such an obvious statement of fact that it hardly seems worth considering. In the peaceful quiet of your bedroom at eleven at night, it is difficult to imagine that any parent, let alone yourself, would ever lie to his or her child. But it happens every day, and one of the reasons that your toddler doesn't understand when you say "No" is that you haven't been telling the truth.

"If you don't stop that you are going to get hurt!" "If you keep that up we are going home." "Okay, just one more story. But this is the last one." "Eat your peas so you will grow up to be big and strong."

Words, words, words . . . They may reflect how you feel, what you are worried about, or what you want to happen, but how many of them convey the truth? Despite your promises, your toddler has climbed up the slide backward a dozen times and has yet to injure himself. Although you have threatened repeatedly, he has never left play group early because he was whining. And although he has never eaten a single pea, every adult he meets tells him how much he has grown.

Many of your words have no relationship to a reality that your toddler understands. It isn't a pretty thought, but you have been lying to your child, and if you want him to understand "No," it is time to start telling the truth.

It will be difficult at first, but try to think about everything you are saying . . . before you say it. What seem like innocuous warnings about little dangers that never materialize accumulate and take their toll on your truthfulness. Young children take what you say literally. Before you utter the words, play them through in your head. Are they really the truth?

Your new, and successful, behavior management plan will be built on truth. We will begin by crafting a set of limits that reflect the real dangers in your child's environment. This will mean prioritizing and focusing your words (threats) on your toddler's most serious misbehaviors and that you stop babbling about the ones that don't require correction. Some behavioral specialists refer to this process as "choosing your battles."

By trimming your threats to the bare minimum, your words will become more effective, but the last and critical step is following your words with consequences that you can administer and your child can comprehend. This is the heart of an effective behavioral management plan, and it is as simple as 1–2–3.

1 Set a limit.
2 Threaten a consequence if the limit is exceeded.
3 Administer the consequence when the threat is ignored.

Once your toddler sees that whenever he goes beyond the limits you have defined a promised unpleasantness occurs, he will think twice about challenging the rules and will eventually abandon the behavior. Initially, he may repeat the misbehavior because he has been accustomed to your inconsistency. It will take him a few days to realize that his parents have changed their ways.

Although the concept of setting limits and administering consequences is simple, it isn't always easy. However, if you have read the first two chapters of this book with an open mind, it will be easier because you have thought about why your child is misbehaving and why it has been difficult for you to say "No." You realize what you may have already suspected: your toddler is basically a good kid, but when he is overtired and/or finds himself in unfortunate circumstances, his behavior degenerates. Bolstered by those exercises in problem recognition and self-examination, it's time for you to get on with the solution.

Learn to Be AUTHORITATIVE

If you are looking for a label to describe the kind of parent you would like to become, sociologist Diana Baumrind has described three styles of parenting that you can choose from. The *permissive* parent makes few rules and seldom administers any consequences when limits are exceeded. This style of parenting may work with a child who is unusually timid and unadventurous, but under normal conditions the result is chaos. Many parents are lulled into using a *permissive* approach when their child is an infant content to lie in his crib or on a blanket on the floor. But limitless parenting is a slippery slope. By the time he is eighteen months old, curiosity and a pair of capable legs have morphed these parents' placid and stationary infant into risk-taking explorer. We have already seen that although most of us prefer to avoid confrontations, your toddler's safety demands some limits. It may be the path of least resistance, but *permissive parenting* is not the way to go.

At the other end of the spectrum is the *authoritarian* parent who makes lots of rules and enforces them strictly. In the short term this approach may keep your toddler safe, but in the long run a child who has very little practice at making his own decisions can flounder when his *authoritarian* parent is no longer standing over his shoulder. As you can imagine, this style of parenting mixes poorly with a child with a natural instinct for exploration, because at every turn he will bump into one of the overabundant rules.

There comes a point in some parent-child interactions when the parent must call a halt to the negotiations and say, "Because that's the way it's going to be." However, the *authoritarian* parent begins and ends *every* conversation with "Because *I* said so!" *Authoritarian* parenting discourages creativity and decision making, and it can encourage rebellion as the child grows older.

Sitting in the envious position between these two extremes of parenting is the *authoritative* style. These parents know that limits are important but they leave their children freedom to explore their environment safely and make some of their own choices. *Authoritative* parents understand their children's temperament and developmental capabilities and create just enough rules to avoid chaos during the toddler years.

They accept that they can never be perfect parents because there is no such thing. However, *authoritative* parents understand that the better they understand their children the closer they will get to perfection.

Start with REALISTIC EXPECTATIONS

Before we begin setting limits and choosing consequences, let's make sure your expectations for your toddler's behavior are realistic. For example, a parent who picks up this book hoping to learn the secret of "teaching" his three-year-old how to sit quietly through an hourlong church service is going to be disappointed.

That probably doesn't surprise you because you already understand that most toddlers lack the attention span or self-control to remain seated in one place for more than half an hour. However, you may have unrealistic expectations for your own toddler. In fact, his natural limit for being stationary and silent may be only ten minutes, and it may be a couple of years before he can tolerate more than half an hour of civilized inactivity.

Unfortunately, the range of normal toddler behavior is so broad that I can't offer you a table or graph against which you can measure your expectations. Your three-year-old niece may be an accomplished sharer of toys and be able to sit quietly waiting to see the pediatrician, while your son rarely shares and usually needs some form of distraction or entertainment to keep him from wandering into strange places. Both children are developing normally, but obviously discipline is going to be a more difficult challenge for you.

If you are concerned about the age-appropriateness of your child's behavior, don't rely on your observations of one or two of his peers. Ask someone who is accustomed to seeing young children on a daily basis such as his day-care provider or pediatrician.

Although I have already told you that there is no such thing as a typical toddler, here are some very general observations that may help you form realistic expectations for your toddler.

Attention span—It is unreasonable to expect a two-year-old to stick to one activity for more than ten minutes. This skill should have increased to about fifteen minutes for a four-year-old, providing that the activity is of sufficient, age-appropriate interest.

The urge to move—Your child spent his first year

trapped in a body that wouldn't take him anywhere. You can expect that while he is a toddler he will want to stretch his legs and explore his environment. The situations you place him in should provide adequate opportunity for physical movement.

Sharing—By the time your child began to walk he understood the concept of "mine," but you can't expect him to share with playmates for another couple of years.

Toddlers are fickle—Items that were favorites one day may be shunned the next. This characteristic is most obvious at the dinner table.

Curiosity—It is unrealistic to expect that a purse left within reach will remain unopened and its contents left without being examined and tested.

Neophobia—Although most toddlers are inquisitive, ironically they are fearful of new places and experiences, including tastes.

Don't Look for TROUBLE
(He Has to Learn Sometime, but He Doesn't Have to Learn It All Now)

One of the deepest traps a parent can fall into is believing that the toddler years are a narrow window in which their child must learn a set of behavioral lessons that she will carry with her into adulthood. Yes, it is important for your toddler to learn that when you say "No" she must stop misbehaving. And, yes, there are principles of social behavior that she must learn before she becomes a civilized adult. But she has another sixteen years to learn them before your parenting responsibility ends.

For example, it is difficult for a toddler to understand that everything within her reach doesn't belong to her. This means that it may take her several years to grasp the concept of sharing. Sharing, like good manners, is something that is best learned by example and not with threats and consequences. Don't look for trouble while this learning process is evolving. If your toddler is having a friend over for a play date, ask her what toys she doesn't want to share and put them away until the date is over. Forcing her to share will make an unpleasant morning for everyone.

Respecting the property of others is a similar concept that most toddlers don't get right away. If Grandma has a porcelain polar bear sitting on her mantel, your toddler may legitimately ask the question, "Can I play with it?" It looks like a toy, and her toys don't break. The answer, "No, it might break," doesn't compute.

"Because Grandma doesn't want you to play with it" is another answer that may not make much sense to a two- or three-year-old. Eventually she will learn that other people won't let her play with things the way you have always done. For the moment the best choice is to put the polar bear out of sight.

> Your toddler is already an expert at finding trouble. There is no reason to enhance the process.

You want your child to respect other people's property, but now may not be the best time to hammer home that principle, particularly if you are still struggling to get her safety-related behaviors under control.

Focus your attention on her safety-related behaviors. Work on keeping your promises and following up on your threats so that your words will be understood and believed. Until you have achieved this, your toddler can learn the more difficult social behaviors by watching your example.

The Answer Is MORE SLEEP

The question is: What is the one thing that you and your toddler must have if you are going to be a happy and effective parent? Sleep deprivation can turn your usually compliant two-year-old into a demon, and it will weaken your resolve to follow through with consequences. While fatigue plays a critical role in the management of toddler behavior, it has received little attention from behavioral specialists. I have always found that oversight surprising because I thought every parent knew that tired children were more likely to misbehave. My mother certainly did. I can recall several occasions when she and I were witnesses to a foot-stomping, rolling-on-the-floor tantrum in the grocery store. My mother would whisper to me, "That poor little boy is so tired. He should be home taking a nap."

None of my medical school professors mentioned the association between fatigue and misbehavior. However, after just a few months of small-town pediatric practice I realized that my mother's advice about sleep was going to come in handy in answering parents' questions about saying "No" to their toddlers. Her lessons to me were just the introductory course. As the years went on I discovered that sleep deprivation could also cause physical symptoms from headaches to leg pain and a variety of psychological problems including depression and distractibility. I also noticed that many parents struggled with discipline issues because they themselves were overtired.

These observations about the importance of sleep have continued to accumulate, and a few years ago I organized them into a book for parents titled *Is My Child Overtired?* Here are some of the highlights that apply to your situation as the parent of a toddler who doesn't seem to understand "No!"

I'M SURE THAT <u>YOU</u> ARE OVERTIRED. I know that you are overtired because survey after survey has demonstrated that most adults in this country aren't getting enough sleep. In a recent survey 56 percent of adults reported regular daytime drowsiness. One sleep specialist has estimated that parents usually lose between 400 and 750 hours of sleep during their infant's first year of life. (*Power Sleep*, James B. Maas; Villard, 1998) This means that you entered your child's toddler years with a substantial sleep debt that you are unlikely to repay in the near future, unless you make some changes in your family's schedule.

IT'S HARDER TO SAY "NO" IF YOU ARE OVERTIRED. It's harder to do everything if you are overtired. Confronting your child's misbehaviors takes energy. After a long day at home or a hard eight hours at the office you just don't have the energy to say "No," even though you know it's the right thing to do.

IT'S HARD TO BE CHEERFUL IF YOU ARE OVERTIRED. In fact sleep deprivation can lead to depression and psychologists know that the children of depressed parents are more likely to have behavior problems.

IT'S HARD TO BE PATIENT WHEN YOU ARE OVERTIRED. There are some situations that are best managed by ignoring your child's misbehavior. If you are sleep deprived you won't have the patience to turn a deaf ear to the sound of your toddler harmlessly banging pots and pans or to walk into the next room when she is having a tantrum.

If you are overtired you are more likely to make threats on which you won't follow up. Even worse, you may lose your cool and strike your child instead of choosing a safer, more effective consequence.

TODDLERS HAVE SPECIAL SLEEP PROBLEMS. Based simply on what their parents tell me I have estimated that 75 percent of my patients aren't getting enough sleep. Toddlers are even more likely to be sleep deprived because they are making transitions from two naps to one and from one nap to none. They start many days sleep deprived because they went to bed the night before without having had the nap they needed.

Driven by their passionate search for independence, many toddlers may refuse to go to bed at a healthy hour.

Others who had mastered sleeping through the night long before they were six months old may begin waking at night for no obvious reason.

TANTRUMS ARE MORE LIKELY TO OCCUR WHEN YOUR CHILD IS OVERTIRED. Like you, your toddler's patience decreases and her frustration level increases when she gets tired. For example, she may play happily with her Legos all morning but at four in the afternoon she throws the entire box of pieces across the room when she can't fit two of them together.

YOUR TODDLER IS MORE LIKELY TO GET INTO TROUBLE WHEN SHE IS OVERTIRED. While sometimes your child acts out to get your attention, many of her behaviors are accidental and the result of risk-taking that has gone bad. Many pediatricians have noticed that overtired children are more likely to have accidents, and a recent emergency room survey has revealed that children seen for trauma had gotten less sleep in the previous day than those who visited the hospital for other reasons.

One of the explanations for this observation is a phenomenon I call *paradoxical hyperactivity*. You may have already noticed that as your toddler gets tired she seems to get a burst of energy before she finally collapses for the day.

Neurologists and psychologists have also found that children become more distractible when they are sleep deprived. The combination of increased activity and a shortened attention span means that your overtired toddler is going to find trouble even when she may not be looking for it.

The bottom line is that if you can keep your child well rested she will have fewer problem behaviors and you will have to say "No" far less often.

YOU WON'T HAVE TO LOOK TOO FAR TO FIND OTHER EVIDENCE THAT YOUR CHILD IS SLEEP DEPRIVED. In case you haven't noticed the association between fatigue and your child's misbehaviors, here are some other signs that your child is overtired.

- She sleeps fewer than twelve hours in a twenty-four-hour day.
- You must wake her in the morning.
- She wants her blanket or security object frequently.
- She sucks her thumb frequently.
- She falls asleep after just a few minutes of a car ride.
- She wakes frequently at night with what appear to be nightmares.

If any of these descriptions fit your toddler, she isn't getting enough sleep and her behavior will improve dramatically after you improve her sleep habits.

WHY AREN'T <u>YOU</u> GETTING ENOUGH SLEEP? I trust you already know how you feel when you are sleep deprived. The harder question is, how are you going to get more sleep? First, you must move sleep higher up on your priority list. Are you staying up to watch television when you could be turning off the light? Have you allowed yourself to become overcommitted to your job or volunteer activities? Has your toddler's bedtime drifted to eight or nine o'clock and left you with little or no time to spend with your spouse before exhaustion overtakes you?

The solutions don't come easily. Can you muster the gumption to ask your boss for a more sleep-friendly assignment? Can you trim your schedule of nonessentials until you get a better handle on toddler discipline? I can't help with those decisions except to guarantee that if you give sleep a higher priority you will be a happier and more effective parent.

What I can help you with is moving your toddler's bedtime to an earlier and healthier hour. The solution to this critical problem can be found on pages 126–131.

Sleep will crop up again in the next two chapters. It is an important factor to consider when you are deciding which of your toddler's misbehaviors deserve your attention first. You will learn some strategies for keeping your child well rested and less prone to misbehavior. We will consider the value of sleep when it's time to choose an appropriate consequence for your child, and I will continue to remind you that if you want your "No's" to be understood you must be well rested yourself.

The Art of SETTING LIMITS

THE BASICS. The next step in building an effective discipline system is creating limits that are appropriate for your child's temperament and developmental stage. While the concept of making a list of rules to protect your child from his environment is easy to grasp, actually doing it can be difficult. If your child stayed in his bedroom twenty-four hours a day, the job would be much simpler. However, he eats in the kitchen, plays in the family room, and brushes his teeth in the bathroom . . . and that is all before eight o'clock in the morning.

Once out of the house your toddler may roam the backyard or neighborhood playground. He may spend more than half his day at daycare, and he may accompany you to the grocery store or mall. Each environment offers its own collection of hazards and temptations and will require its own unique set of limits. To further complicate matters you won't be the only one drawing and enforcing the boundaries. Your child has a mother, a father, and possibly a daycare provider whose limits may not always coincide. These are just a few examples of how complex limit-setting can become. To simplify the process let's strip it down to the basics:

Here is your child:

For the moment he is sitting quietly in a spacious environment free of tempting and dangerous objects. If he chooses to get up and explore, he could do so safely. I know it's hard to imagine such an idyllic environment where a parent never needs to even think about saying "No." But you were there once when your infant was just a few months old and spent much of his time safely confined in his crib or chair.

Things have changed. Your toddler's horizons have broadened and now he exists in an environment that includes a variety of objects:

For purposes of illustration I have chosen six very different objects. Among the temptations is a porcelain *vase* your great-aunt brought back from China in 1930. This heirloom is worth far more to you than its appraised price of three hundred dollars. It has been resting peacefully on one of the lower shelves of your bookcase since you inherited it years ago.

There is also an *entertainment center,* which holds a twenty-six-inch television and your CD player, each with a tempting array of knobs and buttons. Unfortunately, this piece of furniture has no doors. Just around the corner is a bathroom with a gallon and a half of water in the *toilet bowl,* more than enough to drown a curious toddler. In the kitchen nearby is a *stove* with an oven door that can get hot enough to cause a serious burn to the thin skin of your toddler's palm. Under the sink is a collection of toxic *cleaning solutions.* Also in the kitchen is another cabinet full of *pots and pans* that your child likes to bang together. You don't care about them being damaged because they are old, but the noise can be annoying, particularly late in the day.

Without limits in place it will only be a matter of minutes or seconds before your quietly seated toddler is investigating these dangerous temptations. Looking for adventure, he is bound to find trouble sooner rather than later. You could place a playpen in the middle of the family room, but before long your toddler will be agile enough to climb out. Another solution is to erect an invisible boundary by making rules. If you made no changes in the environment, his limits would look like this:

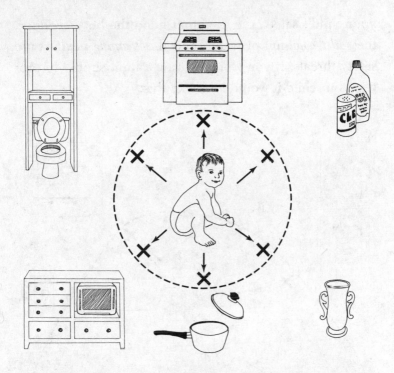

You can see that this arrangement creates at least six opportunities for confrontation (the Xs). "No, you can't play with the VCR." "No, you can't touch the stove." No, you can't pick up Aunt Ethel's vase," etc., etc. If you enjoy confrontations and like looking for trouble, this set of limits is for you.

To make the process more rational and easier to administer, let's divide those tempting items into two categories by asking whether an object is a threat or a potential victim?

It's true your toddler could do some serious and costly damage to the *entertainment center* and *vase,* but the *pots and pans,* the *entertainment center,* and the *vase* pose no risk to your child's safety. On the other hand the hot *stove* door, the *toilet bowl* full of water, and the *cleaning solutions* are safety threats. If you were to draw a limit simply to protect your child it would look like this:

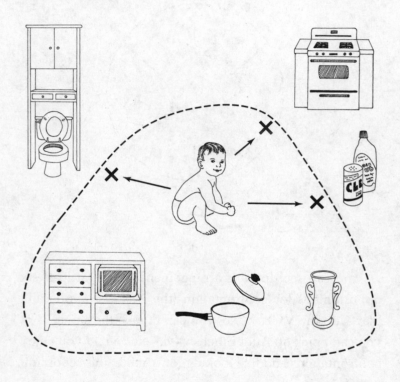

This safety-first prioritization is the strategy you should start with if your child's behavior is completely out of control. It keeps the potential confrontations to a minimum and allows you to focus your energies on the most important issues.

We could also categorize the objects based on how

easily they can be excluded from your child's environment. For example, the *vase* can be packed away in a
trunk in the basement until your child is old enough to understand and respect its value. Of course you could stub-
bornly leave it in a tempting location, but remember there
is nothing to be gained by making the whole process
more difficult than it needs to be.

The *cleaning solutions* and the *pots and pans* could also
be moved out of the environment, but unlike the *vase* they
must be kept close at hand but safely out of reach of your
child. A locked cabinet under the sink is an obvious answer for the *cleaning solu-
tions.* However, locking up
the *pots and pans* is not a
workable solution. Since
their presence in the environment is a threat neither
to your child nor to themselves, we can remove
them from consideration

> **When you don't
> know where to
> start, ignore your toddler's
> nuisance behaviors and
> focus on his safety-related
> misbehaviors.**

by defining them as a nuisance. For the moment, ignoring
the clatter and clang eliminates them from our limit-
setting exercise.

The *stove,* the *entertainment center,* and the *toilet* can't be
moved and so until you can devise a strategy for exclud-
ing them, they will remain as temptations. Fortunately,
the bathroom has a door on it. This allows you to remove
the *toilet* from the environment simply by installing a
hook-and-eye latch on the door. This is an example of

how you can solve discipline problems with a quick trip to the building supply store. *(You will find many other examples in the next chapter.)*

As a result of redefinition *(pots and pans)*, architectural manipulation *(toilet, cleaning solution)*, and removal *(vase)* we have altered your toddler's environment to look like this:

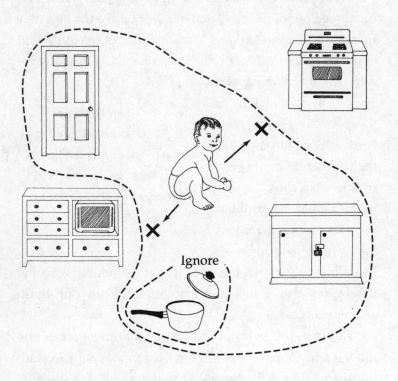

In this simplified example we have manipulated the environment so that the only items that must be excluded by the rules you make are the *stove* and the *entertainment*

center. One is a hazard to your child. The other is a potential victim of his exploration. The new arrangement of his environment means that you will be saying "No" much less often. Now you can focus your parental energy on making a few threats ("If you fiddle with those knobs . . .") and following them up with the promised consequence (". . . you will have a time-out").

Choosing a safe and effective consequence and learning how to make threats that convey your message are the topics for the next two chapters.

ADJUST THE LIMITS TO MATCH YOUR CHILD'S TEMPERA-MENT. When you are setting limits, remember that all toddlers are not created equal. Your niece may be so timid and unadventurous that your sister could confidently leave her unsupervised in a room full of fragile china. However, your toddler may start each morning on a search for adventure that will leave no stone (or anything else) unturned.

This means that the limits you set for your child will look much different than those your sister sets for her daughter. Both of you will include the same basic safety issues such as running into the street or playing with the toxic cleaning materials stored under the sink. On the other hand, when it comes to nuisance behaviors such as noisy play or running in the house, as the parent of an energetic toddler you must think twice about drawing boundaries that are too restrictive.

Placed in an environment with too many rules, the energetic explorer doesn't have to go very far to bump into a limit, and his parent will spend most of his or her day saying "No!" With each confrontation comes another opportunity for a threat and a consequence. If the threatened consequences always happen, these misbehaviors can be kept in check, but his temperament will drive this energetic toddler to continue his search for excitement. Every day will be full of "No's" and "Don'ts." This arrangement isn't much fun either for parent or for child, and eventually wears the parent down until he or she can no longer follow through.

The parent of the less adventurous toddler can erect a very tight boundary without a significant increase in confrontations. For example, she could make a rule that her child is to remain on the six-by-eight area rug whenever he is in the family room. A single sharp reprimand may be all it takes to keep this malleable toddler in place. I suspect it may be hard for you to relate to this situation, but there are toddlers who can be managed simply with a raised voice.

You may be envious of parents with an unadventurous toddler, but they have their own problems. Because their child is unlikely to complain, they may build an unnecessarily restrictive environment that discourages their toddler's curiosity and creativity.

The challenge for every parent is to establish limits that are just tight enough to eliminate their child's dangerous behaviors without creating pointless confrontations or squashing his sense of adventure. I can guarantee that you won't do it correctly the first time, but success will come through trial and error. In fact, you will never be a perfect limit setter. On days that you are overtired, you may be so intolerant of noise and toddler chaos that you make rules to eliminate nuisance behaviors that you could have easily tolerated and ignored the day before when you were rested. There is nothing wrong with that kind of inconsistency as long as you haven't chiseled the rules in stone by using words like "never."

If you are concerned that you have set limits that are inappropriate for your toddler's temperament, ask someone who has more experience with child behavior and knows your child. This could be your pediatrician, day-care provider, a neighbor, or even your parents. I find that when I am asked to consult on limit-setting issues, my advice is usually to loosen rather than tighten the boundaries. Fewer rules, consistently enforced are more effective. This strategy minimizes unnecessary confrontations and encourages healthy curiosity.

THE ARCHITECTURAL PRINCIPLE—The answer to your problem may be waiting at the hardware store. Saying "No" is hard. If you can find someone or something that can make the job easier, don't be a martyr. Accept help wherever you find it. This is particularly true when it comes to setting limits. You already know that your first priority is to create a protective boundary between your adventurous toddler and the dangers in his environment—the busy street in front of your house, for example. This can be achieved with warnings, reprimands, threats, and chasing after him, or it can be done by erecting a physical barrier such as a fence.

> *B*efore you set a limit and make a threat, look for an inanimate object or a structural rearrangement that will make the rule unnecessary.

You already know that using words alone is exhausting, labor intensive, and requires consistency to achieve success. On the other hand, architectural boundaries do all the work for you. A fence says, "No, you can't run in the street" more clearly and more consistently than you can. A latch on a cabinet door doesn't have to listen to whining or back talk, and a gate across a doorway will never be tempted to negotiate or give your misbehaving toddler "just one more chance."

Architectural solutions can be as cheap as a $1.29 hook and eye to keep a bathroom door closed, or as expensive as $50,000 to create a separate bedroom for your child. You will have to decide whether your problem justifies the cost of the architectural solution. On the other hand, spending $5,000 on a fence may not make sense if you were thinking of moving in the near future or were planning on having only one child. By the time your toddler is four or five, you will probably be able to trust him to stay out of the street without constant supervision.

Architectural solutions may not always fit with the decor you planned so carefully in your carefree, childless days. But let's face it, your life has changed dramatically, and like it or not your home is going to reflect those changes. Your friends with children don't expect your home to look like something in *Architectural Digest,* and your friends without children will remain clueless until it's their turn.

You will find examples of "The Architectural Principle" scattered throughout the rest of this book, but I gathered them together and added a few more to help you begin the process of thinking outside the box.

Electric receptacle covers—You should already have these. They cost just a few cents. Shop around and experiment. Some are too easy for some children to remove.

Cupboard latches—If you have dangerous chemicals or valuable articles stored in waist-high cupboards you can install safety latches that require an extra step to open. I have yet to find one of these that will foil every toddler. Before you go to the trouble of installing these on all of your cabinets, do a test installation. You may find that less attractive hasp and padlock arrangement mechanism is required to keep your mechanically minded toddler out of the bleach.

Hook-and-eye latches—These are the least expensive and easiest to install of the door-latching hardware. Chain latches are more complicated and have the disadvantage of allow the door to be opened an inch or more. However, this can be an advantage if you can't bring yourself to close the door completely. Doorknob covers that slip unless squeezed tightly by an adult hand offer another way to keep a door closed, but I haven't found them to be as successful as the old-fashioned hook and eye.

Gates—Folding gates make convenient barriers for

creepers and inexperienced walkers, but when your toddler has learned to climb, it is time to erect more substantial barriers.

Doors—Many newer homes boast an "open plan" with a variety of spaces that are defined by window and furniture placement rather than doors. Sleeping lofts may replace bedrooms. These designs create well-lighted, cheerful, and flexible spaces, though sometimes at the expense of separation and privacy.

You may live in an older home and have removed some doors to achieve a more open feel. Now that you have a toddler it's time to rehang or install a door or two to define your child's space and protect him from danger.

Rearrange your furniture—When doors won't solve the problem or are too expensive, consider rearranging couches, bookcases, and bureaus to create barriers. Furniture lacks the flexibility of a door, but may be a short-term alternative, particularly for an area that you want to be off-limits during the day but available to you after your little explorer has gone to bed. If you use this strategy, make sure that the furniture, particularly bookcases, is secured so that your toddler won't be able to topple them over and injure himself.

Redefine spaces—If you have two children who must share a bedroom, sibling conflicts and sleep issues may be difficult to manage. Is there a way to redefine spaces so that each child can have his own bedroom? Can the computer/office move in with you for a year or two? Can the playroom be converted to a bedroom?

Fences—A fenced-in area in your yard will allow your

child to enjoy the health benefits of fresh air and exercise without requiring you to ride herd. Permanently installed fences are expensive and may not add to your property value. Temporary fences erected with movable stakes and metal or plastic screening can be found at any building supply store and are an inexpensive, albeit unaesthetic, solution.

Bells and buzzers—If your toddler is a night wanderer and you can't bring yourself to latch his bedroom door, sleighbells hung on the doorknob will provide a low-tech warning that he's on the move. If you or your spouse has a yen to tinker, you can find what you need to build a buzzer system at a do-it-yourself electronics store.

Dimmers—If poor sleep habits are contributing to your child's misbehaviors, a darker bedroom may be part of the solution. Dimmer switches are easy to install and can allow you to make a gradual transition to sleep-conducive darkness without an argument.

How to Do Time-Out and MAKE IT WORK

A well-crafted and executed time-out will be your most powerful tool in helping your child to understand what "No!" means. We have discussed why it hasn't worked before. Now it's time to walk through the way to do it correctly. Each step is important and has its own rationale. It's never as easy as it sounds at the start. There will be wrinkles of various sizes, and we will iron these out at the end of the chapter.

MAKE YOUR THREAT. In the next section you will learn exactly how to word your threats and how to warn your child that an appropriate consequence is just around the corner. For the moment let's assume that you have already made it perfectly clear that if your child keeps misbehaving he will be going to his room for time-out, but the behavior continues. It's time for action.

Don't be afraid to let your child know you are unhappy with his behavior, but don't allow your anger to overwhelm the situation. Although it can be difficult to contain your emotions, you will be most effective if you assume a "this is all business" demeanor. A cool, nononsense style will keep you from saying things you will be sorry for later. You can reopen the warm and fuzzy side of your personality when time-out is over.

MAKE YOUR CHILD'S BEDROOM THE TIME-OUT SPACE. I have warned you that using a chair for time-out is labor intensive and fails to create sufficient isolation from you and the temptation for continued misbehavior. If you want time-out to be an effective consequence you must use a separate room.

Like many parents you may be hesitant to turn your child's personal space into a prison. Although using his bedroom as a time-out space could in theory discourage your child from enjoying his bedroom as a haven, in reality it doesn't. My three children and the hundreds of other children whom I have worked with continue to treasure their bedrooms as a personal space even though they have been occasionally forced to retreat there for time-out.

Toddlers may not have a fully developed vocabulary, but they aren't stupid. They understand that the point of time-out is forced isolation. Your child knows that there is nothing wrong with his bedroom just because it is where he stays for time-out. He will continue to treat it as his special personal space.

I have been asked by some parents if it is a good idea to use another room if one is available. My answer is no for two reasons. First, that arrangement can eliminate the therapeutic benefit of time-out, which is that it offers your overtired child a chance to fall asleep. Second, time-out is not intended to be punitive. Your child need not suffer to benefit from time-out. Separation is the point behind time-out, not depravation. There is no reason your toddler shouldn't be in a place he is familiar with, surrounded by his toys.

TAKE YOUR CHILD TO HIS BEDROOM. This may mean simply telling your child to go to his bedroom, but it may require taking him by the hand and walking him into his room. If your child objects or is having a tantrum, you must pick him up and carry him. This is the "physical" part of time-out.

I understand that this may be difficult for you, even though you are still three times bigger and stronger than your toddler. Carrying a thrashing toddler to his bedroom isn't a pleasant experience. But it can be done, and it must be done if time-out is going to succeed. If you are consistent in following up every threat with a consequence, the physical struggles will become less frequent and violent and will eventually disappear. Once your child realizes that the consequence is inevitable he will accept it more readily.

To make the job easier, scoop your toddler up from behind in a firm "bear hug." The more of his extremities you can tie up in your arms the less flailing there will be. There is a good chance that you will take a few heel whacks to the shin. Ignore those for the moment. We will come back to a suggested response in the next section.

REMIND . . . BRIEFLY. While you are taking your child to his room, you can remind him *in one sentence* why he is being sent to his room. "I asked you to stop playing with the CD player because it might break." This should not signal the start of a dialogue, argument, or negotiation. Do not answer questions or respond to counterthreats and requests for another chance. Your statement is merely a reminder and is not a necessary ingredient of time-out. If your child is screaming, he isn't listening anyway.

STATE AND RESTATE ONLY ONCE THE TIME-OUT SENTENCE. "I want you to stay in your room quietly for three minutes"—one minute per year of age. "I will start the kitchen timer as soon as I hear 'quiet.' When you hear the beep, you can come out."

If you start the timer before your child has quieted down, the misbehavior is still ongoing and the consequence will be much less valuable. Waiting for silence will give you both time to cool down and make a repeat of the initial scenario much less likely.

CLOSE THE DOOR. This is a critical step in making time-out work for two reasons. First, it emphasizes the separation between the warmth and approval of your family circle. If the door is left open the isolation is incomplete. Closing the door increases the power of the consequence. It is a clear signal that you take the misbehavior seriously.

Second, the closed door makes it easier to follow the next step, which is to remain silent. If the door is open, you may give in to temptation and start a dialogue with your child during his time-out.

MAINTAIN YOUR SILENCE UNTIL THE TIME-OUT IS OVER. This part is difficult because you would like the consequence for your child's misbehavior to be over almost as much as he does. However, reminding him after the door is closed that you won't start the timer until he is quiet won't speed the process along. In fact repeating the message will defeat your goal of removing your approval. We want to create the illusion that in one sense you are miles away, but will return in the blink of an eye when the consequence has been completed and your child's behavior is acceptable.

It may help you to think of the often cited behaviorist principle that even negative attention will reinforce negative behavior. By remaining silent you are removing all attention, both negative and positive.

"I'm thirsty," "I have to pee," "I'm sorry," and "I won't do it again" all must be ignored. Your child can hold his urine for three minutes and certainly won't become de-hydrated waiting for the timer to beep. The thumps and bumps of toys being thrown and closet doors being slammed must also be ignored, and they delay the start of the timer. When your child is in time-out he must understand that your ears are tuned to hear only silence. Obviously, if the noises coming from your child's bedroom suggest that he or his room are in danger, you must intervene. These situations do occur and we will deal with them in the last section of this chapter.

WHEN YOU HEAR SILENCE, START THE TIMER. Silence here is a relative term. If your child is talking to himself, singing, or his toys are making their usual noises, that is as good as silence. If screaming, whining, banging, or stomping resumes, you must reset the timer.

USE YOUR CHILD'S TIME-OUT TO CONSIDER WHAT YOU COULD HAVE DONE TO PREVENT HIS MISBEHAVIOR. I advise that you use your child's room for time-out so that you both can have a time and a place to cool off. Take advantage of the opportunity. Were your expectations for your child's behavior unrealistic for someone of his age and temperament? Did you allow him to get overtired? Was your timing off? Could his activity been scheduled at a time of day when he was better rested? Was he getting enough attention? Were there too many other children and distractions?

Had you allowed yourself to get overtired? If you had been better rested would you have been more patient? If the answers to these questions suggest that you threatened too hastily, don't worry. We all make mistakes. In the next chapter we will look at how you can repair these human errors. But for now, you have threatened time-out and you must carry through with the consequence if you are going to maintain your credibility.

WHEN THE TIMER BEEPS, OPEN THE DOOR AND OFFER YOUR CHILD A BIG HUG AND A KISS. This act of forgiveness welcomes your child back into the fold. He has returned to a place where he can receive your attention and approval.

This is not a time to ask for apologies. The consequence has been completed and the misbehavior forgiven. Your warm and approving behavior signals to your toddler that you know he is basically a good kid and you love him. You can speak the words too if you wish, but a hug is all he needs. This welcome back to the rest of the family also emphasizes the basic principle of time-out, which is separation, and sharpens the distinction between inclusion and exclusion.

DON'T REHASH THE MISBEHAVIOR. When your child has completed his sentence and you have given him a big hug, it's time to get on with your lives. There is nothing to be gained by sitting your child down and reviewing the misbehavior that prompted the consequence. He knows what he did wrong. The discussion is going to make only you feel better because it will give you one more opportunity to state your position. Your toddler heard you the first time, he just didn't believe there would be a negative consequence to his behavior. Now he does.

TREAD GENTLY THE FIRST TIME. The guidelines that I have outlined may be a radical change from the way you have been administering time-out. Your child doesn't know you have been reading this book and doesn't realize that he is dealing with a new and more decisive parent who will follow up every threat with the promised consequence.

He will be surprised the first time you scoop him up in your arms, carry him to his room, and close the door behind you as you leave. Our goal isn't to scare your child into behaving properly, but leaving him alone in his room with the door closed can be frightening, particularly if it has never happened before.

The first time you decide to use your child's room for time-out, shut the door for only ten or fifteen seconds. You may need to hold the door shut if he tries to open it. Reenter the door if your child seems frightened. Sit down with him on his bed and tell him that you are sorry he is afraid, but he must understand that if he misbehaves there will be a consequence and this is the one you have chosen. Tell him that he can leave his room now, but if he misbehaves again, he must return and it will be for "a much longer time."

If the next time you use time-out your child's reaction is the same, wait another fifteen or twenty seconds before you open the door. Repeat the process, continuing to increase the time with each episode. If your toddler is genuinely frightened by being alone in his room, your threats of time-out will stop his misbehaviors once he understands you mean business. It is more likely that as the time intervals increase you will discover that it is frustration and not fear that is driving your toddler's response to being alone in his room. For the moment, suspend the rule that your toddler must be quiet before he can leave his room. You can reinstitute it once you are comfortable that time-out isn't terrifying your child.

What Can Go WRONG?

Though time-out may work like a charm the first time you send your child to his room and shut the door, it is more likely that you will have to endure a shakedown period that takes several days. Here are some adjustments you can make to make time-out fit your family's situation.

YOUR CHILD PLAYS HAPPILY IN HIS ROOM WHILE HE IS SERVING HIS TIME-OUT. It may be a difficult concept to accept, but this scenario is not a problem and is surprisingly common. Remember, that our goal for time-out was to stop the misbehavior. It was not intended as a painful punishment that must be endured.

When your child is in his room playing quietly you should be happy because the misbehavior has stopped. He's doing what he wants to do and so he's happy. Because you made a threat and carried it out, the consequence will still have some deterrent effect. This is one of those hard-to-find win-win situations.

YOUR CHILD'S BEDROOM DOESN'T HAVE A DOOR. You can try using a folding gate, but most children over the age of eighteen months have figured out how to climb over or dismantle them. If your child can still be safely restrained by a gate, remember that you must keep out of sight and remain quiet to make the feeling of isolation more complete.

> Administered properly, time-out in your child's bedroom will not interfere with the good sleep habits that you may have worked hard to instill. The child who has mastered independent sleep understands the difference between the separation that occurs each night at bedtime and time-out.

The better, although more expensive, solution is to install a door. I told you that many of the answers to your behavior management questions would be found at the building supply store. This is a prime example. If your child is going to understand what "No" means, the buck must stop somewhere.

YOUR CHILD DOESN'T HAVE A ROOM OF HIS OWN. Select another room that you can make safe or close off. You may have to move some furniture and redefine the purpose of other rooms in your home. For example, if you have a study or den with a door, you could temporarily move your computer, television, and collection of sports memorabilia into your bedroom.

Some parents use their own bedroom for time-out. Obviously, this arrangement can only work after you have gone through drawers and closets to make sure that all dangerous or valuable objects have been removed.

If you live in an open-concept house in which the bedrooms are lofts and walls and doors are few and far between, there may not be a room that can be isolated. If this is the case, you can try to use a time-out chair providing visual isolation with drapes or screens and being careful to be quiet. Obviously, this situation doesn't work very well if your child is unwilling to stay in the chair.

While remodeling your home to create a room for time-out sounds like overkill, your child is going to request a private space sooner or later. If you are perilously close to the end of your rope and have tried everything you can think of to get your child to understand "No," the cost of remodeling will be a good investment.

YOUR CHILD TRIES TO DESTROY HIS ROOM. If the tirades are limited to a little toy-tossing and foot-stomping that results in nothing more than some cosmetic damage to the walls and woodwork, they are best ignored. To keep the damage to a minimum, take off your child's shoes and carry the heavier toys out of the room with you when you leave.

Some parents have told me that when their toddler was in time-out he would pull out bureau drawers and scatter clothes around the room. This stunt can be foiled by turning the bureau so that the drawers face the wall.

However, it is probably easier to ignore the mess and silently clean it up when the time-out is over. Although you may be tempted to add on another three minutes to the consequence or make him clean up the room himself, remember that we want to keep this process simple.

When your child is in time-out, he is alone in his own environment; as long as he quiets himself for the allotted time his sentence has been paid. Your ears must stay tuned to hear only the sounds of silence, and you should ignore those relatively harmless bumps and thumps. If you are worried that he may do serious damage to his room or himself, the next section contains the answer.

YOUR CHILD'S TANTRUM SEEMS TO GO ON FOREVER. One answer to this situation is simply to wait him out. It will eventually stop. It might be forty-five minutes or an hour, but if you can keep quiet, it will stop. However, if you break the rule of silence and try to shorten the tantrum with unsolicited advice, you are prolonging a dialogue in which you are talking and your child is screaming.

Although waiting out a severe tantrum will work, there is a more humane approach that can shorten the torture for you and your child. If it is becoming obvious that your child's tantrum is not going to stop after a few minutes, reenter his room and encircle him in your arms in what one pediatrician has termed the "Big Hug." Be careful to protect yourself from flailing arms and legs. Tell your toddler once that you are going to hold him until he settles down, but don't begin a conversation.

Wrapped firmly in your arms, your child will calm

down in just a few minutes. The tantrum may end with a string of deep sobbing breaths or a sound sleep. When the fireworks are over, explain to your toddler that now that he is quiet you are going to leave him alone to finish out his sentence. Without telling your child, subtract a minute from his time-out.

This technique is strictly optional, but once you see how it can shorten the unpleasantness, you will want to use it for severe outbursts. It's the nice thing to do, and it doesn't reinforce more violent tantrums.

YOU ARE INJURED BY A FLAILING LEG OR FIST AS YOU CARRY YOUR CHILD TO TIME-OUT. This happens. You may be tempted to add another minute or two to the time-out, but don't. Keep your anger in check. Losing your cool isn't going to help your child's behavior. Bite your tongue and promise yourself that next time you will be more skillful in scooping up your writhing toddler. To do otherwise will confuse the simple message of time-out: one consequence for one misbehavior.

Remember that you are dealing with a little child who hasn't learned addition and subtraction. There is nothing to be gained by keeping a tally of misbehaviors.

YOUR CHILD OPENS THE DOOR AND ESCAPES. This is by far the weakest link in most parents' time-out strategy. I've lost count of how many families have told me that time-out hasn't worked because their child won't stay in his room. The answer is obvious and simple, but like many simple solutions, it isn't always easy to accomplish.

If your child won't stay in his room, you need some way of keeping the door shut. Some parents try to do this by holding on to the doorknob. This technique can work, but it usually doesn't. Your child knows that although you are on the other side of the door you are still connected to it. Even if you can remain silent, this doorknob tug of war is just another, albeit nonverbal, way of communicating with your toddler. If you are holding on to the door, you haven't achieved the complete separation that makes time-out work.

The better solution is buy a hook-and-eye latch at the hardware store for $1.79. It takes five minutes to install and will allow you to walk a few steps into another room confident that your child will stay in his room. I know that there are many parents who have trouble accepting the idea of latching their child inside his room. They may feel that by securing the door that they have become one of those horrible and demented parents who lock their children in rooms or chain them to radiators for days, weeks, or even years. Remember, I am suggesting a time-out that lasts only minutes, and I am certainly not recommending that you leave the house while your child is latched in his bedroom.

Some parents are hesitant to take such a definitive step, but that is exactly what you must do if your child is going to understand what "No" means. The buck must stop somewhere. There must be a bottom line, or consequences have no teeth and threats are just idle words. Latching the door is such a simple way of saying enough is enough. It can be done humanely, by using the gradual approach I described on pages 98–99.

Most parents find that they no longer need the latch

after the first few episodes. In fact time-outs become less frequent because the child begins to respond positively to warnings and threats. The hook hangs idly on the door frame as a reminder that when you say "No" you mean the behavior must be stopped or there will be a consequence that can be neither negotiated nor escaped.

Latching a child's bedroom for time-out is a strategy that many pediatricians have recommended for years. However, few have written about it because the technique lacks a certain political correctness. I have been criticized by a few parents who have heard that I recommend "locking misbehaving children in their rooms." What these critics have missed is that latching a bedroom door for time-out is the final and often unnecessary step in a comprehensive approach to behavior management that emphasizes prevention.

Putting a latch on your child's bedroom door is a humane, sensible, and effective way of making sure that your child understands what you mean when you say "No." I hope that this book will be read widely so that more parents will discover this simple and safe solution.

Threats and WARNINGS

CHOOSE SOME NEW WORDS. Now you have a safe, effective, and therapeutic consequence to use when your toddler challenges the limits you have tailored to fit her temperament. The next step is re-scripting your threats to match the new discipline plan you have created. If you wish, you can continue to use the old words and phrases that have lost their meaning after months of misuse. It won't take too many trips to her bedroom for your child to realize that "No" means "Stop what you are doing *now!*" However, you can speed the learning process by unwrapping another set of words and putting the old tarnished set on the shelf. In a few months of rest, you will be able to return "No" and its abused partners into circulation. They will sparkle as though they were brand-new because now they will always be followed by a consequence.

For example, if your standard threats have included *No, I mean it, I'm not kidding, I'm getting angry, Mommy doesn't like it when you . . . Please stop,* give them a rest. They have temporarily lost their meaning. Replace them with a simple "If you do that again, you will go to your room for time-out." Of course, if the behavior is repeated, you *must* follow through and take your child to her room. You can reiterate the time-out rules as you close the door if you wish, but at that point no more words are necessary. Don't waste them.

CRITICIZE THE DECISION, NOT THE CHILD. To help nurture and preserve your child's self-image avoid describing *her* as "naughty" or "stupid." It is better to focus on the misbehavior by saying "That was a bad choice" or a "I'm surprised that a smart little girl like you would do a dumb thing like that."

NEVER SAY "NEVER." To help your words retain that golden ring of truth, avoid absolutes such as "never." The threat, "If you ride in the street again, you can *never* get on that tricycle again" will come back to haunt you. Within a week you will have to retract your threat or spend a long afternoon listening to your three-year-old whine that she has nothing to do. It is a mistake that we all make, but if you want your child to understand and believe what you say, promise yourself that you will never say "never" again.

TOO MANY CHANCES . . . <u>TWO</u> STRIKES AND YOU'RE OUT. You may have been giving your child too many chances to correct her behavior in the past. Until you feel comfortable that your child really understands that every threat will be followed by a consequence, and you are prepared to act on the very next incident, don't make any more threats. Of course this means that you must choose your words carefully when your child misbehaves. There may be situations when you would like to issue a warning (see next section), but when it is time to make a threat, there should be no second chances. Strike one: "If you hit your sister again, you will go to your room." Strike two: The child hits. Now you must remove the child. In baseball the rule may be three strikes and you're out, but when it comes to helping your toddler understand "No," the second strike means time-out.

This "two-strike" rule may sound overly strict to you, and in the long run it is one that I don't expect you or any parent to follow in every situation. There are occasions when you would like to give your child a third or even a fourth chance to correct her behavior, but I assume that you have been reading this book because you are having trouble saying "No." Until you regain control of the situation and are comfortable that your toddler understands that you mean what you say, the two-strike rule should be in effect.

WARNINGS . . . BUT NOT TOO MANY. Although the essential ingredients of a good discipline plan are limits, threats, and consequences, timely warnings can allow it to function more smoothly. A warning alerts your child that she has entered a danger zone. Unlike a threat it does not state a consequence, but it may imply one.

A warning can offer the rationale behind the limit you have set. "I want you to stop playing with that because . . ." and "If you climb up on that you might fall and hurt yourself" fall into this category. When you have issued this kind of warning before you threaten the consequence, there is no reason to repeat it as you walk your child to her bedroom for time-out.

"Your whining is making me angry" is another kind of warning. It alerts your child that you are reaching the end of your rope. While it may not be very specific, it is informational without suggesting an imposed consequence.

Although warnings can put a stop to some misbehaviors before they reach the point of requiring a consequence, they lose their effectiveness if overused. One (two on a bad day) warning per misbehavior should be sufficient. After the second unheeded warning, you can be sure your child isn't paying attention. You should never have to ask, "How many times have I told you not to . . . ?" Listen to other parents and you will hear how infrequently they follow this suggestion. Six, eight, ten warnings may precede a threat that may not be followed by the promised consequence. Even the most patient eavesdropper may be tempted to finally blurt out, "Please stop dragging this out! Either remove your child from the situation or make a legitimate threat and follow it up with a consequence."

Remember that our goal is to have your child understand that you mean what you say. Following up on your threats is the most important way to achieve this, but keeping your words to a minimum will increase their value. Repeated warnings will only annoy the other adults in the room; your misbehaving child has tuned you out long ago.

COUNTING TO TEN. Some misbehaviors such as running into the street are discrete and must be managed by a threat that begins, "If you do that again . . ." On the other hand there are misbehaviors that are more continuous in nature, such as refusing to come in the house for lunch. Because they are usually less dangerous than discrete misbehaviors, you can manage them with a counting threat.

For example, "I'm going to count to ten. If you aren't sitting at the table when I get to ten, you are going to your room for time-out." If "ten" is always followed by the promised consequence, a counting threat will become one of your most powerful discipline strategies. Many parents, including my own, have been using this technique successfully for years.

I like counting because it provides your toddler an opportunity to mull over the situation. While you are counting she is weighing her options, and ultimately she will make a decision and then must accept the consequences of her decision. She will begin to feel part of the discipline process and view the consequences you impose as something over which she has some control. Although you may have seen a time-out coming, it may seem like a lightning strike out of the blue to your toddler. Counting threats can minimize these unpleasant surprises.

Your child doesn't have to know how to count to understand a counting threat. I have seen the strategy work with nine-month-old infants. Most eighteen-month-olds can play ring-around-the-rosy. They know that after "ashes, ashes" everyone falls down, and they will quickly learn that after nine comes ten and after ten comes a trip to their bedroom.

You can choose a magic number for each occasion or you can stick with one number and change the speed of your counting to fit the urgency of the situation. I happen to prefer five, but I encourage you to choose a number that is ten or less.

Remember that a counting threat is also a warning and as such can suffer from overuse. If your child stops the misbehavior when you get to eight, but five minutes later you hear yourself counting again, it is time to stop counting and issue a final threat. "If you start that again, you are going to your room."

CHOICES. Many child behavior specialists suggest that you offer your toddler choices when you want him to stop misbehaving. For example, "Zachary, I don't want you to play with that vase. It will break. Would you rather play with this dump truck or read a book in my lap?" Theoretically, offering choices is a good strategy.

The problem comes when parents work too hard at finding appealing alternatives for their child. The situation may not offer any safe choices or you may not have the time to go hunting for them. Thinking up good choices for your toddler may require more creativity than you can muster at five o'clock in the evening after a long, hard day at home or at the office. On the other hand, some parents go overboard and offer too many choices. In the section on food-related misbehaviors (pages 162–166) we will examine the deep recesses of this pitfall in more detail. Even adults are overwhelmed when faced with too many alternatives. Two choices is all that your toddler needs to make a good decision.

If no safe and appealing alternatives are readily apparent, offer your child the choice between stopping the misbehavior and an appropriate consequence. A well-crafted threat will include all the information he needs to make the correct decision.

Consistency . . .

(When It's Critical and When It Isn't)

"If you want your child to behave, you must be *consistent.*" You have heard it a hundred times, but what kind of consistency are we talking about? Does consistency mean that you and your spouse must establish the identical limits and administer identical consequences? Does it mean that you and the daycare provider must be working with exactly the same rules? Are you being consistent if you allow your toddler to run in the house in the morning, but forbid it in the afternoon?

The answer to all of those questions is "No!" Of course it is inconsistent for one parent to allow a behavior and the other to forbid it, or for you to make a rule in the morning and retract it in the afternoon when you are too tired to enforce it. Those inconsistencies are a fact of life and your toddler already understands that different places and different people have different rules.

In Chapter 4 you will learn how to expand your behavior management plan to include two parents, a daycare provider, and even several grandparents. In that chapter I will emphasize the importance of communication and coordination, but consistency between the various participants is impossible and a goal not worth pursuing.

However, there is another kind of consistency that is critical to helping your toddler understand "No." That is the consistency of doing exactly what you say you are going to do. Whenever you or anyone makes a threat or a promise to your child, it *must* be followed by the promised consequence or reward. The failure to consistently speak the truth will undermine all of your other efforts to improve your toddler's behavior.

You can move bedtimes, reinstitute naps, and draw temperament-appropriate limits, but as long as you continue to issue warnings that aren't followed by threats, and threats that aren't followed by consequences, your child will ignore what you say. Day-to-day and person-to-person consistency is nice when it can happen, but consistency in keeping your promises and following up your threats with action is absolutely essential to managing your child's problem behaviors.

Correcting YOUR MISTAKES

WHAT TO DO WHEN IT'S TOO LATE TO BITE YOUR TONGUE.
All parents says things to their children that are regretted as soon as they have left their mouths. Whether it is issuing a threat for a trivial misbehavior that could have been ignored or choosing a consequence that is too severe, we have all let our tongues slip when we were exhausted or distracted.

How can you extricate your child and yourself from these unfortunate situations without seriously damaging your credibility and eroding the foundation of the discipline system you have worked so hard to create? Again, the first step should be a backward one. Take a long, hard look at the situation. What can you do the next time to prevent a similar scenario and avoid the ugly breach that you are now trying to repair?

For the moment, that is water over the dam, so don't get distracted by going on a guilt trip. The next step is to, at least, initiate the consequence you have threatened. To do otherwise will tarnish your credibility. However, as long as you don't make a habit of it, there is nothing wrong with abbreviating an excessive consequence.

For example, your three-year-old has just ridden her trike into the street for the second time this afternoon. You shriek, "That's it! I'm putting your trike in the basement for a month!" Before the sun has set you realize that this consequence is far too long and is going to make life miserable for everyone in your family.

The solution is to endure the sentence you have given yourself for a day or two. When you can't take it anymore, choose a quiet moment (when she isn't begging to ride her trike) and sit down with your child. Tell her, "I know I said that you couldn't ride your trike for a month, but I realize now that I made a mistake by choosing such a long time. When you rode into the street yesterday I was so scared and angry that I didn't think enough about what I was saying. You can have your trike back this afternoon, but I want you to remember how upset you made me. If it happens again, I'm sure I will mean it when I say, 'No trike for a month.' "

The keys to this approach are that it is honest, it allows you to express your feelings, and you come across as a caring parent and not some autocratic dictator who makes arbitrary rules and exacts harsh and excessive punishments. You have apologized, corrected your position, and your words still have meaning.

When Things GET UGLY

There are several behaviors that are so dramatic that they deserve their own discussion. The basic principles of behavior management still apply, but in the turmoil of the moment you may have difficulty remembering them. The better you understand these ugly episodes, the better able you will be to respond to them rationally and effectively.

TANTRUMS. These outbursts can be as simple as screaming fits or as complex as roll-on-the-floor, foot-kicking, door-slamming theatrical extravaganzas. They are unpleasant to watch and in some ways remind me of a seizure because the tantruming child is irrational and the event may end with sobbing respiration and a deep sleep as after an epileptic fit. Like seizures, they are more likely to occur when children are overtired. Fortunately, unlike seizures, tantrums don't pose any threat to your child's health.

As dramatic and ugly as they may be, the best advice regarding tantrums is to ignore them. Trying to rationalize with your tantruming child won't work because he probably isn't listening and is unlikely to make sense if he does speak. Your actions (or inactions) remain your most effective method of communication.

Walking away from your child who is pitching a fit can be difficult if you are concerned that he might hurt himself or damage something with his thrashing. You really don't need to worry that your toddler will injure himself during a tantrum, but if it makes it easier for you to ignore, move him to a safer place. The best choice is his bedroom because your response can easily evolve into a time-out. This is particularly appropriate because many tantrums end with sleep.

While your child's tantrum may not have begun as a ploy for attention, the more you become involved, the more likely it is to continue. You may have already observed that tantrums seldom occur when your child is in the care of strangers. This may be because he suspects that his extraordinary behavior won't be tolerated unless you are present.

Another tactic is to use the "Big Hug" that I described on page 102. Encircling your child in your arms will calm him, prevent him from hurting himself, and shorten the tantrum. Don't be surprised if he falls asleep in your lap.

HEAD-BANGING. Some children include head-banging as part of a complex arm-swinging, foot-thrashing tantrum. More often it is simply something your child does when he is frustrated, either because you won't allow him do something, or he can't figure out how to do it.

As you can imagine, this is a very difficult behavior to ignore, particularly if your toddler chooses to bang his head on the hardwood floor of the dining room. Nonetheless, ignoring is still the best approach. *Your child will not damage his brain by head-banging.* He may develop a bruise and the skin over his forehead may become temporarily thickened and discolored, but his body is programmed to stop banging well before he damages his brain.

Another approach is to pad the bars and ends of your child's crib with blankets (this may require some duct tape). After a few episodes, you will be able to anticipate when a confrontation is going to prompt a bout of head-banging. Scoop your child up and place him in the padded crib. He will receive much less physical gratification from banging on a padded surface, and of course you are less likely to worry.

Don't confuse head-banging done in anger or frustration with the rhythmic head-banging that some normal children (and adults) do to relax and/put themselves to sleep. This self-pacification is not a behavior that requires a response on your part. However, if it is occurring frequently, it is another message that your child is overtired.

BREATH-HOLDING. Breath-holding is the most frightening behavior a parent will encounter. You may have heard adults threaten in jest, "If you don't stop, I'm going to hold my breath until I turn blue and pass out." But in nearly thirty years of pediatric practice I have never seen or heard of a child holding his breath on purpose. Now, I have certainly seen scores of children hold their breath to the point of unconsciousness when they were upset. In fact I was a breath-holder and have a daughter who did it occasionally when she was a toddler. But in every case it was an accident of nature, a peculiarity in the child's physiologic response to fear or anger.

When children prone to breath-holding spells take their first extra deep breath in anticipation of letting out a scream of fear or anger (but in most cases it's fear), their respiratory control system gets stuck on the "in" phase. Their skin begins to turn blue as the oxygen level in their blood declines, and if the process goes on long enough, their oxygen-starved brain loses consciousness. In some cases these children may twitch for a few seconds as though they were having a brief seizure. As you can imagine, this scenario is not a pretty sight. Fortunately it usually lasts less than a minute, and the loss of consciousness solves the problem as the child's respiratory system jump-starts itself into action. (There is another, less common, form of breath-holding spell in which the child's heart rate slows down dramatically and instead of turning blue, the child becomes ashen.)

As frightening as these episodes appear and as un-healthy as "oxygen starvation" might sound, breath-holding spells, even repeated ones, do not cause brain damage. Once the spell has begun there is nothing you can do to stop it. You must wait the few agonizing seconds it takes for the process to run its course. Blowing in your child's face or sprinkling water on him (apparently my mother doused me with an entire glass on one occasion) will do no good.

I expect you to call your pediatrician in a panic the first time your child has a breath-holding spell. It is the natural and logical response. He or she will ask you some questions but probably won't need to examine your toddler before giving you the reassurance that you are hoping for.

If your child is a breath-holder, it can make saying "No" more difficult because you know that every now and then your threat or promised consequence may trigger that first exaggerated deep breath that begins the ugly scenario. As hard as it may be, don't let your child's breath-holding spells deter you from creating sensible limits and administering appropriate consequences. Remember, the spells aren't causing brain damage, and once the child has begun crying, the spell is over and is unlikely to return during this confrontation. Once your child has revived and been given a brief comforting hug, it's off to time-out or whatever consequence you have threatened.

After a few of these episodes you will become skilled at predicting when they are likely to occur. This may make tolerating them a bit easier for you, although you will never feel comfortable watching your child turn blue. Well-timed and carefully issued warnings may prevent some breath-holding spells, because they are more likely to occur when children are surprised. Remember, too many warnings without a threat or a consequence will undermine your credibility.

BITING. Biting is probably the most serious crime your toddler can commit. It is a behavior that can destroy friendships, and if persistent, may get your child expelled from daycare. If your toddler has a reputation as a biter, other parents will think twice about inviting you when they are organizing play groups or planning backyard cookouts.

Infants are oral little people. They express themselves with their mouths. You may have fostered this mode of expression by exchanging affectionate nibbles. It is not surprising that when things aren't going his way, a toddler, whose verbal skills are still developing, will respond by biting.

You must make it very clear that this method of expression is unacceptable. Biting him back (a strategy often recommended by aunts and next-door neighbors) is a bad idea. It seldom works, and it merely promotes the notion that when we are upset it is okay to bite.

The better strategy begins by examining the situation in which the biting has occurred. Is your child overtired? Are there too many other children in a small space? Has his place in the pecking order at daycare been usurped? Do what you can do to correct the situation, and then turn your attention to choosing an effective response the next time he bites.

Immediately after the bite, pick your child up with your eyes burning with a glow of anger he has never seen before, and yell into his face, "DON'T YOU EVER DO THAT AGAIN!" If your act has been successful, he will cry while you are taking him to his crib, room, or time-out space for thirty seconds of time-out. Don't wait for him to stop crying before you end this mini time-out and remind him again how angry you are. This may strike you as an excessive response bordering on verbal abuse, but remember that biting is an ugly and serious crime and your failure to take effective action promptly may result in the destruction of your relationships with other families.

If you have managed to play the role of a wild-eyed irate parent well enough, this method works very quickly. If it doesn't, investigate the potential causes again and work on your acting.

If the biting is occurring at daycare and not at home, this is a problem for the daycare provider to manage herself. There is little you can do at home to stop the behavior. You can offer suggestions about napping, staffing, and organization and condone her efforts at administering appropriate and timely consequences.

CHAPTER
4

Putting Your Plan
TO WORK

How to Say "No!"
AT BEDTIME

SAFETY FIRST, BUT SLEEP IS A CLOSE SECOND. Sleep deprivation is the most frequent and preventable cause of toddler misbehavior, and it is now time to put your newly acquired limit-setting skills to use in getting your child the sleep she needs to be well behaved.

While your toddler's dangerous misbehaviors should receive your attention first, her sleep schedule should be next on your list. Bedtime refusal, repeated night wakings, and giving up naps prematurely are among the more difficult behaviors to manage, but when her bad sleep habits have been corrected, many, if not most, of your toddler's misbehaviors will disappear. Let's bite the bullet and tackle your toddler's sleep problems at the same time you are reining in her most dangerous behaviors. It won't be easy to find the patience and stamina at a time of day when you're tired, but remember that your successes in sleep management will make the rest of your parenting chores easier.

> The time and energy you invest in correcting your toddler's sleep habits will pay the biggest dividends.

Because your child should already be in her bedroom, time-out won't work with sleep schedule problems. However, there are simple solutions that rely on the same principles we have covered already. Let's look at some strategies for getting your toddler the sleep she needs to be well behaved.

SLEEP REFUSAL—HOW TO SAY, "NO, IT'S BEDTIME." The most difficult sleep issue to deal with is bedtime refusal. It is also the most important, so let's deal with it first. Begin by calculating your toddler's healthy bedtime. A two-year-old should be getting thirteen hours of sleep in twenty-four hours, and a three-year-old needs twelve. Subtract her nap time and then count back from the hour she wakes in the morning.

For example, a two-year-old who takes an hour-and-a-half nap and wakes at 6:30 in the morning should be falling asleep at 7:00 at night. To complete the calculation, subtract the time it takes to complete her bedtime ritual. If it takes a half hour to brush her teeth, read a story, and say her prayers, you must start the process at 6:30. This may sound unreasonably early to you because over the last thirty years North Americans have allowed their children's bedtimes to creep later and later. We have arrived at a point that many parents believe they are doing a good job if they have their toddlers asleep by 8:30.

Getting your family rounded up, fed, and ready to begin your toddler's bedtime ritual at 6:30 or 7:00 may take some serious rescheduling and re-prioritizing. Do what it takes, and you will be pleasantly surprised at the benefits. Begin by trimming your meal preparation time. Young children don't eat much later in the day. Consider moving bath time to the morning. Make sure that your child's afternoon nap is early enough so that she is appropriately tired at bedtime (see pages 134–135).

If one parent's work schedule prevents him or her from arriving home in time to be part of the bedtime ritual, it should take place without him or her. Your child's sleep is more important than it is for her to see both of her parents at bedtime. Quality time for a toddler is usually in the morning. A few minutes of family-bed before breakfast is a better trade-off if you can't be there for bedtime.

You can allow for a little slippage in schedule on the weekends, but you must realize that we all have trouble resetting our biological clocks when Monday rolls around. This is particularly true for children, and going to bed more than an hour later can spell trouble. In fact, for some children even a half-hour change will send a well-crafted sleep schedule into a tailspin.

Once you have set an appropriate bedtime, you are ready to craft a ritual that is sleep-promoting and efficient. This means avoiding vigorous physical play for the hour before bedtime. Many fathers look forward to a little friendly tussling with their children at the end of their workday. Unfortunately, this rough-housing can wind up your toddler and delay her bedtime beyond a healthy hour. Reading or watching a video or TV show in the family room is usually a better choice, but avoid subject matter that might be frightening or too stimulating. Do not allow a television in your child's bedroom. Several studies have demonstrated that TV sets interfere with healthy sleep patterns.

Set clear limits on the number of bedtime stories. If your child pleads for "just one more," you may want to draw a pictogram of her bedtime ritual and tape it onto her bedroom door as a reminder.

Your toddler may complain that she is afraid of the dark. Plug in a *small* nightlight in a wall receptacle near the floor. Too much light is a significant deterrent to good sleep patterns. If she demands a brighter light, install a dimmer in the switch (even I have mastered this simple home-handy-person challenge) and gradually decrease the light over a period of two weeks. If she wants the door open, agree to leave it open, but just a crack.

If monsters are the problem, monster hunts before bedtime only serve to validate her concern that they exist. If there aren't any monsters, then why would a parent go looking for them. Tell your child that there are no monsters and agree to sit in a chair by her bed until she falls asleep. Lying down with her will perpetuate an association that is difficult to break. Over the next week, gradually move your chair closer to the door until you are sitting in the hall. Eventually, you will be able to stand in the hall for a few minutes or not at all. This weaning process can be time-consuming, but as long as you stick to your plan it will work.

Requests for drinks of water or trips to the bathroom can be ignored because these were elements of the bedtime ritual. If it makes it easier to turn a deaf ear, leave a spill-proof cup of water and a potty chair in the bedroom, but these are unnecessary frills that distract from the real issue. Your child just doesn't want to go to bed alone and miss out on the family fun she imagines will carry on without her.

Once you have set the limits for your toddler's bedtime ritual, you must be prepared with consequences when she balks. If she leaves her bedroom after the ritual has been completed, escort her back to bed, tuck her in, give her a kiss on the forehead, and leave. Do not agree to repeat any of the bedtime rituals.

Walk her back to her room as many times as your patience and stamina allow. When you have reached the end of your rope, it's time for a consequence. You can begin by telling your child that tomorrow night's bedtime will be fifteen minutes earlier if she leaves her room after the bedtime ritual has been completed. You can also threaten to eliminate one of her favorite elements of the ritual tomorrow. These threats are generally not as effective with toddlers because the consequence is too remote from the misbehavior. It's likely that either she or you will forget twenty-four hours later.

Threatening to turn off her nightlight and/or shut her

bedroom door are much more effective threats because they are immediate, definitive, and very unpleasant. However, these consequences must be administered carefully. Being closed in a dark room can be very frightening, particularly for a child who is already anxious about making the transition to sleep by herself. The first time you make the threat and are forced to follow through, turn off the light or shut the door for no more than five seconds. This is usually enough to demonstrate that you mean what you say. If you haven't already used the moving-chair technique (see pages 128–129), offer that option to your child. If she comes out of her room after you have given her a second chance, close the door or turn off the night-light for an additional ten seconds (this means total dark time of fifteen seconds). I will be very surprised if this second response doesn't stop the behavior, but if your child is very persistent, continue to increase the dark time as you would with a time-out.

If your toddler stays in her room but attempts to extend the bedtime ritual simply by calling out, issue one verbal reminder that it is time to fall asleep and then ignore her. Ignoring is difficult late in the day, but it will work. Save the lights-out/door-closed consequence for the situations when she actually leaves the room.

Don't worry if your toddler ends up sleeping on the floor. That is her choice. Even in Maine, where I live, a toddler will stay warm enough in winter wearing a blanket sleeper. If she feels cold, she can, and will, build herself a nest with the blankets from her bed. She will be fine until you check on her as part of your own bedtime ritual a few hours later.

MIDDLE-OF-THE-NIGHT WAKING—HOW TO SAY, "NO, YOU CAN'T SLEEP IN OUR BED." We all wake at least once or twice in the middle of the night, but those of us with good sleep habits will simply change position and allow ourselves to fall back asleep. We may not even open our eyes. However, if your toddler believes that you are an integral part of the sleep process, you will hear from her when she wakes, whether it is ten at night or two in the morning.

This means that the first step in dealing with middle-of-the-night wakings is to make sure that your toddler's evening sleep ritual does not include lying down with you until she falls asleep. The second step is to understand that the more tired your child is, the more often she will wake at night. I know it doesn't sound logical, but it's a fact. This means that you may need to move her bedtime earlier and/or re-institute her nap.

If getting her more sleep doesn't completely eliminate her middle-of-the-night waking (and it usually doesn't), the next step is to promptly return her to her bed as soon as you discover her standing next to your bed. This re-bedding ritual should be no more than a businesslike pat or kiss on the forehead. No trips downstairs for a drink. No stories and no videos.

Continue to return her to her bedroom as long as you have the stamina. It may take several weeks, but it will work. Don't cave in and let her crawl into bed with you.

If your toddler is sick, accompany her to her room and hold her in your lap as long as she wishes. This may be more uncomfortable for you, but keeping your bed off-limits at night will prevent an annoying habit from developing (see the section "How to Say 'No' When Your Toddler Is Sick"). A few minutes of "family bed" time in the morning is fine, but be sure to draw limits that define how early is too early (see next section).

If your child is so quiet and you are so tired that you don't wake when she crawls in, then attach some old sleigh bells or a similar noisemaker to her bedroom door to alert you that she is up and prowling.

If your child is healthy and her continued reappearances in your bedroom have pushed you beyond your limit or you don't hear the noisemakers you have installed on her door, it is time put up a gate or latch on her door to keep her in. If the idea of latching your child in her room at night sounds unsafe to you, consider this: The risk of house fire is very small, but the chance of serious injury to a toddler wandering around the house unsupervised is much greater.

Follow the same process of brief door closing and lights-off that I described in the last section. If you can remain consistent, this technique will be effective after a few days, two weeks at the longest. While you are working to curb your toddler's night waking, you will probably start off each day sleep deprived. Look at your schedules and find a week when you have a minimum of other responsibilities and can afford to be less productive. The week(s) that you invest in improving your child's sleep, and ultimately yours as well, will be time and energy well spent. Your well-rested child will have fewer misbehaviors, and as a better rested parent you will be more tolerant and consistent.

THE TOO-EARLY RISER—HOW TO SAY, "NO, THIS FAMILY DOESN'T START ITS DAY AT 5 A.M." Your toddler may slumber off at night without a whimper and sleep without interruption until five o'clock when she wakes ready for action. You may be tempted to accept this as an unpleasant but natural behavior of a child who doesn't need that extra one and a half or two hours of sleep. However, most early risers finish their day exhausted and cranky. They really do need to sleep longer in the morning. This is why a later bedtime is not the solution.

Repeatedly walking your early riser back to bed doesn't work either because by the time you have done it enough times to be effective, the rest of the family is ready to get up. The best approach is a combination of ignoring and compromise.

If your child stays in her room and calls to let you know she is awake and ready to play or eat breakfast, don't respond. If she ventures out, you may need to resort to threatening to latch her door. Of course, these strategies aren't going to get you any more sleep in the short term, but once your toddler understands that there is no alternative but to stay in her room, she will accept it.

It will make things easier if you can compromise on a slightly earlier wakeup time for the entire family. Install one of those security timers on a light in the hallway outside your toddler's room. Set it to turn on a half hour before you are ready to get up. The light is a signal to your child that she can come into your room for a half hour of family bed time (remember she can't tell time). Morning is quality time for most well-rested toddlers. Breakfast is often their best meal of the day. Getting up a half hour earlier can turn it into a relaxed family event instead of a rush-for-the-lifeboats escape from the house.

LOST NAPS—HOW TO SAY, "NO, YOU'RE TOO YOUNG TO GIVE UP YOUR NAP." One of the things that can make your two-year-old terrible is the loss of her afternoon nap. There are two strategies you can use to prevent the premature loss of your toddler's afternoon nap. The first is to weld it to her midday meal so that it becomes her *after-lunch nap*. Making this firm association has several advantages. First, it takes advantage of the natural drowsiness that occurs after a midday meal. You may not have noticed it if your child has been allowed to play actively after lunch, but sleep researchers tell us that early afternoon is a time when her body is programmed to fall asleep.

Second, by attaching your toddler's nap to her lunch, she will be less likely to give it up as she gets older. She is never going to give up her lunch, and if she has become accustomed to napping after lunch, the habit will persist longer. Furthermore, an afternoon nap that doesn't begin until 2:30 or 3:00 will mean that your toddler is not appropriately tired at her healthy bedtime of 7:00.

Finally, when your child is programmed to nap after

her lunch, you can dictate when she naps by moving her lunch earlier or later. For example when she is beginning to drop her morning nap and lacks the stamina to make it through an entire morning, you can give her lunch at 10:45 or 11:00 in the morning, and she automatically gets an early nap. You can use the same strategy when her behavior tells you that she is getting sick.

Even if you weld your child's afternoon nap to her lunch, there is no discipline strategy that can make her sleep. All you can do is create a sleep conducive environment and say, "No, you aren't going to do anything else but sleep or rest." This means that as your toddler gets older, you can label her *after-lunch nap* a *siesta*. Don't make appointments, turn down rings on the phone, and eliminate stimulating toys and activities for the hour after lunch. Offer to sit on your toddler's bed and read her several soporific stories, or join her on the couch for a bland video or show, such as *Mister Rogers' Neighborhood*. On the days that she is very tired, your toddler may nap during her *siesta*. If she doesn't, and is obviously exhausted by late afternoon, the solution is an earlier bedtime.

PACIFIER RULES—HOW TO SAY, "NO, YOU CAN'T WANDER AROUND WITH YOUR PACIFIER IN YOUR MOUTH." Some behavioral specialists refer to pacifiers, favorite blankets, and stuffed toys as "security" or "transition" objects. While they can comfort in frightening or painful situations, blankets and pacifiers are primarily sleep aids. On most occasions when your toddler asks for her pacifier she is telling you that she is tired.

One simple rule can prevent overuse of your toddler's pacifier or blanket while preserving both its comforting and sleep-enabling functions.

> "You can have your pacifier* anytime, but you must be in your room to use it."
> (*or blanket or special stuffed toy)

Your toddler is intelligent enough to understand that this rule is not the same as time-out, but it helps if you present it with the proper emphasis. It is not a consequence or punishment, but simply an acknowledgment that everything has its place. When we feel that we need to use the toilet, we head for the bathroom, and when we are feeling tired, our bedroom is the place we go.

Like every rule, it has some important exceptions. If you are going on a long car ride (something of an hour or more) during which you hope she will sleep, the pacifier can come along. At daycare, "bedroom" can be replaced by "sleeping mat."

If you are headed for a situation that may be painful or frightening, such as a trip to the doctor's office, the pacifier should go along in your purse or pocket for rapid retrieval. If your toddler injures herself at home, accompany her to her room and offer to sit on her bed with her (and her pacifier). When you sense that the crisis has passed and you are no longer needed, ask if she minds if you leave. Remind her that the pacifier must stay in her room, and that you will return immediately if she wants to cuddle some more.

Pacifier use has been linked to ear infections and dental deformities, but incorporating this rule in your behavior management plan will prevent these consequences. It will also help you and your child realize when she is tired and encourage her to make the appropriate choice. When she is tired, she will take herself to her bedroom instead of misbehaving.

"But DADDY Lets Me . . ."
(One Child, Two Parents, and Three Sets of Rules)

One of the most difficult things about helping your child understand "No!" is that it is often a shared task. Unless you are a single parent, you will have to contend with complaints that begin with "But Daddy (or Mommy) lets me . . ." It is the unusual family in which both parents can agree on every limit and every consequence in every situation. In fact, I bet it has never happened. Human nature dictates that we each look at the world from a unique perspective and therefore have our own personal threshold for misbehavior.

You may not allow your toddler to bounce on the bed, but your husband might. On the other hand, your husband may tell your child that he must finish his peas or he won't get dessert, while you don't believe in conditional desserts. These discrepancies are bound to occur, and if not dealt with promptly and appropriately, can damage your marriage. At the very least they are unsettling to your child and will make it very difficult for you to create an effective discipline plan.

It won't take long for your toddler to seize on the opportunity this provides. Even though it may be a year or two before he whines, "But Mommy lets me . . . " he will begin to attack the point of least resistance—the parent most likely to have the more lenient set of limits.

> You and your partner must have a plan for managing the situations in which you disagree about a limit or a consequence.

First, you both must agree that disagreement is normal and inevitable. You and your partner may have voted for the same candidates in the last election and you both may take cream in your coffee, but that doesn't mean that you must agree on a response to every one of your child's behaviors. Diversity of opinion is what makes the world go 'round.

Second, you must realize how unsettling it is for a child of any age to hear his parents argue. My parents seldom raised their voices at each other, but I can still remember the hollow emptiness I felt the few times it did occur. Your toddler understands that his parents may not always agree, but he relies on both of you for support and stability. A disagreement that has heated up to the point of becoming a full-fledged argument can shake his confidence in the underpinnings of the family. He doesn't know it will blow over by morning.

DIFFERENT SITUATIONS MAY HAVE DIFFERENT RULES. Even two-year-olds can understand that each circumstance can come with its own unique set of limits. For example: "If I'm home alone with Dad, it's okay to use my bed as a trampoline. But if Dad's still at work and Mom's in charge, I'm not allowed to do it." If you think you can explain differences like this to your toddler without sounding judgmental, you can try. But I think you'll find it's better to simply leave it as a statement of fact.

These differences in tolerance are just one of life's realities that your child should learn when he is young. When he gets to school each of his teachers will make his or her own set of rules for classroom behavior (and some may not make much sense). He must learn to adapt his behavior to each teacher's rules if he is to succeed in school. As a twenty-something adult, he must understand that the things he says and does when he is at a comedy club with his friends may not be acceptable with his co-workers at the office.

There are many limits that you and your partner can agree on easily. Obviously, your child will not be allowed to play with matches or run into the street. However, there are many behaviors where there is room for disagreement. Bouncing on the bed is a good example because it's dangers are less universally appreciated. (Bed bouncing is actually quite dangerous. In my experience, beds have caused more cuts and broken bones than trampolines.) It is perfectly reasonable for each of you to have drawn your own limit regarding bed bouncing that applies when you are home alone with your child.

The problem comes when you are both at home with your child. Whose limits should guide your child's behavior. One option would be to create a combination of Mom's and Dad's rules. Because there are dozens of minor issues on which you and your partner may differ, the composite boundary will be very confusing for your child—and yourself—and therefore I don't recommend it.

The Better SOLUTION

FIRST, MINIMIZE YOUR DIFFERENCES. To differ is human, and your child can learn to love and respect your differences, but the more uniform your boundaries, the better. Sit down together *after* your child has gone to bed and is out of earshot and try to resolve as many discrepancies as you can. These discussions (and there will be more than one) should take place when you are both rested and willing to talk. This could be at home in the evening or it could be an agenda item for a dinner date. Ask your friends with children how they have handled similar issues. Your pediatrician can also serve as an arbiter, particularly when one of you feels that your child's health and safety are at stake. In my busy practice I take on this role on the average of once a day.

Even after you have questioned your consultants and

had your discussion, differences of opinion will remain. I hope these are so minor that each of you can feel comfortable allowing your partner to set and enforce his own set of limits when he or she is alone with your child. If this is not the case, it's time to call a family counselor or mediator to help resolve the conflict. You may feel awkward about hiring a consultant over what may seem to other parents like a minor matter, but from these little sparks full-fledged fires of discontent can erupt.

STEP BACK AND BITE YOUR TONGUE. You and your partner may agree that you can each have your separate rules when you are alone with your child, and I have warned you that a composite set of limits is too confusing. This means that when all of you are together one of you must step forward as the voice of authority and the other parent must step back and bite his or her tongue.

It makes the most sense if the parent setting the limits is also the one who is better at following through with consequences. The arrangement also requires that the other parent maintain silence even though he or she may not agree with the boundary that has been drawn. You know as well as I that keeping quiet when you disagree with something, particularly when it involves your child, can be extremely difficult. But it isn't impossible and when it comes to managing your child's behavior, it is essential.

If your partner has already told your child that it is time to go to bed, and your child asks to read one more story, you must be able to say convincingly, "No, it's bedtime." Even though you may not see any harm in reading another story. Resist the temptation to use phrases such as, "You heard what your father said," which could be interpreted as, "but if you had asked me first, I would have read you another story." As difficult as it may be to step back and play a supporting role, your ability to bite your tongue will pay big dividends when it is your turn to set the limits and dispense with the consequences.

One of you will probably take the leadership role more often. Strong relationships are not formed by joining exact equals. Successful marriages balance one partner's strengths against the other's vulnerabilities. If you are the parent who has more difficulty following through with consequences, accept your role as bystander. You may be the favorite story-reader or Band-Aid applier, but you may not be the better disciplinarian. Your child will understand and appreciate the advantages of this cooperative arrangement.

On the other hand, if neither of you is willing to step forward to draw a line in the sand and follow through with consequences, then anarchy will reign. It won't be pretty, and it certainly won't be in your child's best interest. If you both have trouble sounding and being authoritative, take turns at assuming the role of disciplinarian. In this case, the silent partner's quiet can be supplemented with nods of approval.

There may be occasions when the usual rule-maker and consequence-distributor is not up to his or her job.

When this occurs, your child will understand if he is told, "Mommy's too tired to answer that question right now, but I think it's okay for you to have another handful of goldfish crackers before dinner." However, when Mommy has finished her nap and is ready to pick up the mantle of discipline again, she must not second-guess her partner's decision when her toddler says he's not hungry for dinner. Any debate on the issue should be held later that night after the child has gone to bed.

In a perfect world, your child would have two parents who always agree on where limits should be drawn and how consequences should be administered. It ain't gonna happen! The best that we can hope for is an arrangement in which you agree to disagree and to discuss those disagreements when your child is out of earshot. That is an attainable goal and one which you must achieve if you are going to be successful parents.

Public APPEARANCES
(How to Say "No" When You're Not at Home)

What can you do when your child misbehaves at a restaurant or in the checkout line at the grocery store? A tantrum is guaranteed to draw a crowd in any public place. While some bystanders will glower at you because your flailing and screaming child is making a shambles of their long-planned quiet evening with good food and a nice bottle of wine, most of the crowd will politely pretend not to see or hear the foot-stomping and whining. But everyone will be listening to hear how you are going to manage the situation. You can be sure that your success or failure will be discussed and debated once you are out of ear shot. "I'd never let my child get away with that kind of behavior." "Have you ever seen such a spoiled brat?" "Those poor parents. They don't seem to have a clue." Or, "Wow, I've got to try that with my own kids."

There are few moments that are more embarrassing than when your child acts up in public. You can try to explain to anyone who will listen that your toddler is usually well behaved and that she had gotten overtired at playgroup earlier in the day. While some people may be sympathetic, many are muttering under their breath, "Why doesn't she just take the little brat home?"

It is a helpless feeling. You may even be tempted to give your toddler a little swat to show your audience you are in charge. If you are accustomed to using time-out, your child's bedroom is at least fifteen minutes away, leaving you up the creek without a good consequence.

The best advice I can give you is to heed the unspoken suggestion of the bystanders who want you to take your misbehaving toddler home. When the situation allows you to escape, Do it! Even if it means leaving a half-empty shopping cart in the grocery store or an unfinished meal on the restaurant table. Your family can survive until tomorrow without that jug of milk you thought you needed. The chances of salvaging these ugly public appearances are slim. Behavioral eruptions are most likely the culmination of a bad day that isn't going to get better without a good night's sleep or a nap.

Many parents press on and ignore the handwriting on the wall that says, "This is neither the right time nor the right place for my child." Don't be stubborn. Cut your losses and head for the restful and more easily controlled environment of home.

Obviously, there are circumstances in which you can't simply drop everything, grab your child, and head home. We will come back to those more difficult situations at the end of this chapter. First, let's look at how you can avoid these public displays in the future.

YOUR TODDLER MAY NOT BE READY FOR EXTENDED PUBLIC APPEARANCES. It isn't easy to accept the fact that your child lacks the stamina or maturity to handle the challenges that come with extended trips out of the house. Your niece who is six months younger may have been an angel at the family reunion picnic last month, and your best friend's son who is the same age as your child always joins her for all-morning shopping trips without a whine. These children are exceptions. Most toddlers can't tolerate extended public appearances without their behavior eroding.

Your child may require more sleep than her cousin, and your child may get whiny and oppositional when she is tired, while your niece curls up peacefully in her mother's lap when she runs out of steam. Obviously, her response to fatigue is acceptable in public, and your daughter's is not.

Your toddler may not be mature enough to accept the concept of sharing with other children at the family picnic or understand that she can't have a bite from every bag of cookies on the grocery store shelf. It doesn't mean that she is never going to develop these social skills, nor does it mean that there is anything wrong with her or wrong with your parenting technique. Some infants walk when they are nine months old, other perfectly normal children don't take their first independent steps until they are fifteen months. Your child may be a little slower than some other children at picking up social skills, but it will happen. Know your child and avoid situations and public places that she isn't equipped to handle. These are likely to end with whining, confrontations, and tantrums. Or venture out tentatively but be prepared to leave if things start going downhill.

The final stumbling block between your child and successful public appearances may be the fact that you still aren't sure that she always understands what you mean when you say "No." Setting limits and administering consequences is more complicated and therefore more difficult when you are out in public. Once you have mastered the techniques in the quiet privacy of your own home, you are more likely to enjoy a good performance when you take the show on the road. Later in

> **Don't try saying "No" in public until you have mastered it at home.**

this chapter you will read how you can *bluff* when you are out in public. But to make this strategy work, your child must believe that every one of your threats will be carried out. It will take several months of consistent consequences at home before you can attempt this deception.

Waiting for maturity to come and waiting for your threats and warning to be effective can be frustrating because it puts you and your child on a short leash. There will be places that you would like to go and events you would like to attend, but your child isn't ready to handle them. You may be concerned that your child will miss out on some important educational experiences if you don't expose her to these events. Don't worry, there will be plenty of opportunities for your toddler to experience the rich fullness of a social life outside the home. Her time will come. Taking your toddler to an event or into a situation that is overwhelming isn't helping her self-esteem.

Get accustomed to declining invitations to events that your child can't handle. It isn't an admission of failure, it is the obvious, sensible, and polite thing to do. I promise that the few clueless people who may interpret your refusal as evidence of poor parenting will be outnumbered tenfold by the rest of us who respect your wisdom and appreciate your courtesy.

SCHEDULE APPEARANCES WHEN YOUR CHILD IS WELL RESTED. I warned you that we would return often to the relationship of fatigue and misbehavior, and here it is again. For example, a grocery store tantrum that occurred at 11:30 in the morning could have been avoided if you had started your shopping trip at 9:00, when your child was well rested and more compliant.

Keep your outings short and focused. Your schedule will be more toddler-friendly if you go to the grocery store first and save less critical errands for later in the morning so that they can be abandoned when your two-year-old begins showing signs of fatigue.

Although most toddlers are more rested early in the day and begin to fade as lunchtime approaches, your child may function with a different biorhythm. She may be at her best after her afternoon nap. You can eliminate emotional meltdowns and tantrums if you schedule your day to have her out in public when she is at her best and resting comfortably at home when she is tired.

Dining out with your toddler is another example of a situation in which many parents overestimate their child's tolerance for fatigue. Those of us with grown children cringe when we see a family with a toddler follow the restaurant hostess into the dining room where we have just settled in for quiet meal. We know that nine times out of ten we are going to witness a social disaster. At eight o'clock the poor toddler is already up past his healthy bedtime and his patience is wearing thin. On a good day at home he is good for about fifteen minutes at the dinner table. That means that he is ready to get down and play (or better yet, go to bed) just about the time the appetizers are being served.

Of course, there are a few young children who can tolerate an hour-long meal in a restaurant at eight or nine o'clock at night. In fact your toddler might have been able to cope with the situation when she was an infant by nodding off peacefully in your lap or in a high chair. But now she is a toddler, and you are courting disaster by taking her out to eat at any restaurant that takes longer than ten minutes to serve food.

If your own parents have temporarily lost their long-term memory and offer to take everyone out to dinner at a nice restaurant, politely suggest that you and your toddler will enjoy the evening more if they stay home and treat you to a night of baby-sitting.

If they really want to share a meal with you and their grandchild, suggest a 5:30 reservation at a family-friendly restaurant. Take-out from a favorite place is another great alternative.

KEEP THE OUTINGS SHORT. Even if your toddler is well rested, her attention span is shorter than yours. She may be happy with an activity or an environment for only twenty minutes on a good day, assuming of course she is involved in something that interests her.

Just because the three other toddlers in her play group can handle two hours together, it doesn't mean there is anything wrong with your child if she has had enough of group play after half an hour. When you try to stretch her beyond her limits, she only has a few ways of expressing her discomfort with the situation. If you have missed the early signs of fatigue, her misbehaviors may escalate from whining to biting and a full-fledged tantrum. You can plan outings that last an hour or two, but they should include several changes in activities and location to hold your child's interest.

WILL THERE BE TOO MANY STIMULI AND TEMPTATIONS?

Even if your toddler is well rested, the public environment you have chosen may be too stimulating. When offered a tempting array of activities or objects, many young children have trouble containing their behavior. An example of this phenomenon is the grocery store checkout line that displays candy at toddler height. Fortunately, many stores have listened to parental complaints and replaced the Tootsie Rolls with the less tempting choice of six sizes of flashlight batteries. But to some children anything in a small package at grabbing distance is as tempting as candy.

You can't take most toddlers through the toy department of a store without expecting them to at least ask to play with one of the toys. It's more likely that they will want to bring one home. Even if you have already decided that you are going to buy your toddler something, you risk a confrontation when you don't buy the more expensive toy that she has discovered.

The recent trend toward mega-stores has made the problem worse. It is difficult to find a pharmacy or hardware store that doesn't sell toys. Eventually, your child will understand that a store is different than home and that she can't have or touch everything she sees, but until you have been able to make this distinction clear, you should avoid these tempting environments, particularly when she is tired.

Your toddler may also have difficulty tolerating large groups of children and/or adults. She may be shy or intimidated by the hubbub and cling to your leg for the whole event. Or she may become so caught up in the excitement that she loses sight of the behavioral limits she readily accepts when she is at home. Impulse control is one of those skills that doesn't come naturally to toddlers. They will learn with time, but the chaos of a public event may push them beyond their capability to cope. The bottom line is that you must be honest about your child's ability to tolerate the level of stimulation you expect at the public event you are considering.

If she is hesitant to participate in an activity, don't push. If she leaps into the action, watch for signs of overstimulation and cool things down by restructuring the situation. You may have no other choice than to leave the event long before you had planned.

LEAVE YOURSELF AN ESCAPE ROUTE. Regardless of how well you schedule your toddler's trips out in public, you must prepare for when your well-knit plan unravels. Little children aren't predictable. Well-rested children who are offered a variety of activities can suddenly become tired or overstimulated when you aren't expecting it. Sometimes an incubating illness can be the cause of the unexplained meltdown.

A prudent parent should always have a Plan B ready when things turn sour. For example, most three-year-olds enjoy the color and spectacle of a wedding, but you must expect that a long ceremony may not hold your toddler's interest. Scout out the church in advance. Where are the exits? Are there any quiet rooms in the basement with toys where your toddler can rest or play when she has had enough wedding for the day? If you are part of the wedding party, assign a trusted relative or hire a baby-sitter to escort your toddler. Provide specific instructions about where they can go and provide them with enough toys to ride out the storm.

Remember that any outing with your toddler may need to be terminated at a moment's notice and well before you had hoped it would end. It's just a fact of toddler parenthood.

FINDING A PLACE FOR TIME-OUT. Although your child's bedroom is the optimal place for time-out, there are other options when you are away from home. If you are visiting friends or family, ask your hosts if you can use a bedroom. Examine the room to make sure it is safe and don't leave your child alone in a room if she is prone to destruction while she is serving time-out.

Obviously, time-out is not as effective when you must stay in the room with your toddler, but it is better than no time-out at all. At least your child will be separated from a situation that triggered the misbehavior. If your child is having a tantrum, this is the place to give her a "Big Hug" (see page 102) and a time for you both to cool down.

If there are no rooms with doors, go outside and sit on the porch or on the backyard swingset if the weather permits. Your car can also be an effective time-out space when you are away from home. It is quiet and your child's tantrum can wind down in relative privacy. However, under no circumstances should you leave your child in the car alone. Sit next to her in the backseat until the time-out sentence is over.

BLUFFING. Otherwise known as "gambling on your credibility," bluffing is not a strategy for novices, nor is it a technique that should be used capriciously. If you have been compulsively consistent in following up your threats for several months, your child not only understands what you mean when you say "No," but she also believes every word you say. Your consistency has been rewarded with a power that you can use judiciously when you are out in public and are tempted to make a threat but can't follow up with the promised consequence.

For example, you have driven an hour and a half to visit your brother and his family for the day and your three-year-old begins to whine and misbehave, creating an unpleasant atmosphere for everyone. Although leaving is an option, it's at the absolute bottom of your list. However, you could threaten to pack up the family and return home, if your child continues to misbehave. Obviously, you are taking a risk that your toddler will call your bluff. If she does, this will seriously erode your credibility if you don't climb back into the car immediately. This means that you must be very confident that your words have that ring of truth that you have been working for months to achieve.

If you have underestimated your child's resolve to continue her misbehaving, you can continue the bluff by putting your child in her car seat and driving around the neighborhood once or twice before issuing one more warning, hoping that this charade will turn the trick. If it doesn't, and you have lost the bet, you must make your promised departure. You may realize when you arrive home that your toddler has a temperature, and your unscheduled exit was the best option.

There is no getting around it, bluffing is just a euphemism for lying, and it should only be used as a last resort in the most unusual situations. You frequently hear parents trying this tactic in grocery stores and shopping malls. It doesn't work for them because they have abused the strategy. Most of their threats have never been followed by consequences and their child knows it. But bluffing can work for you because you have worked hard to keep your promises and follow up on all your threats.

How to Say "No" When
YOUR TODDLER IS SICK

Even sick children misbehave, but obviously it is sensible, correct, and humane to relax the rules and give your child the benefit of the doubt when he is ill. However, loosening boundaries doesn't mean that you should stop following up your threats. Limits can be quickly reestablished once your child is well again, but the damage done by unkept threats and promises will be much more difficult to repair. It is always important to consider the impact of your words before you threaten a consequence, but it is critical when your child's ability to comply is impaired by illness.

If setting limits and following up with consequences has been a challenge when your child is healthy, it will be even more difficult to say "No" when your toddler is sick. Fortunately, many young children become less adventurous and oppositional when they are ill. In fact for some parents the first clue that their child is sick is that he is uncharacteristically willing to sit in their lap and listen to an entire story. For these children, discipline may be a nonissue while they are ill. However, if you have one of these toddlers, you have already learned that in a few days he will be back to his old tricks and you must be ready to reinstitute the limits and consequences that worked before he took sick.

Some young children become more belligerent and confrontational when they are sick. This change is typically the result of the fatigue that accompanies most illnesses. Until you realize that your toddler's misbehavior may be an early symptom of illness, you may have embarrassed yourself by raising your voice in anger, only to discover an hour later that he has a temperature of 102°F.

How far should you bend the limits and when is it time to return to business as usual? There are no absolute answers to these questions, but you must accept that there may be circumstances in which your child's misbehavior demands a consequence, even though he isn't feeling well.

We expect sick children to be whiny and cranky, and as a compassionate parent you are going to ignore these harmless but annoying behaviors that might have warranted a trip to time-out the day before. However, if your three-year-old throws one of his heavy, sharp-edged trucks at his little sister, that behavior demands a response, even if he has been up all night vomiting. You may decide to cut him a little slack because he is sick and merely issue a stern warning, although the same behavior might have earned him three quiet minutes in his bedroom if he were healthy. If there is a second offense, even your sick child deserves a consequence, but you might consider shortening the sentence. Your child's safety and the integrity of his surroundings must still be protected regardless of how poorly he feels.

"NO, YOU CAN'T SLEEP IN OUR BED EVEN THOUGH YOU ARE SICK." One of the most frequently encountered limit-bending scenarios involves where your sick child sleeps. Healthy family sleep habits include everyone staying in their own beds, but sick children with fevers naturally want to be cuddled by their parents. You may be tempted to welcome your feverish toddler into your bed in the middle of the night. However, I suggest that you say "No," because to do otherwise risks starting a bed-sharing habit that may be very difficult to undo after the illness has passed. A better option is to offer to cuddle your child in a chair in his room. You will get less sleep in the short term, but the strategy comforts your child and has little risk of creating a habit that will leave you sleep deprived in the long run.

"NO, YOU HAVE TO TAKE THIS MEDICINE." If your child's illness requires medication, you may be faced with an unavoidable confrontation. Although pharmaceutical companies try to make medicine palatable for children, they aren't always successful. Even when they do succeed in creating a flavor that the majority of children and adults accept readily, your toddler may be in the minority.

Before you begin what may become a messy and ugly struggle, be sure that your child really needs the medication. There will be times when forcing your toddler to take medicine will feel like you have slipped over the fine line between physical discipline and abuse. If you aren't convinced that the medication is necessary, you will give up before the dose has been administered.

Your failure to follow through will mean that your child doesn't get the full benefit of the medication, and it will tarnish the credibility we have been trying to establish. You began by saying, "This medicine is important and you must take it!" When your child resisted, you changed your tune. "Well, it really isn't that important. We can forget it for now." If that is your message about the first spoonful of medicine, the chances your toddler will accept a second dose are slim to none.

Before you leave the pediatrician's office make sure that you understand why he or she has prescribed the medication. Ask what will happen if the medicine isn't taken.

Are there alternative therapies? Unfortunately there are situations in which physicians (myself included) prescribe drugs because we sense that's what parents are looking for. If you ask, you may learn that there are safe and effective alternatives that don't involve forcing medicine into your unwilling toddler. Doing nothing might be the best option.

Make a clear distinction between optional over-the-counter medicine and prescription drugs that must be taken. For example, there is no reason to force your child to take cold remedies. They are generally ineffective and may have bothersome or even dangerous side effects. The recent discovery that cold remedies containing phenylpropanolamine can increase the risk of stroke should be a somber reminder that even a medication that has been around for many years may have as yet unappreciated side effects.

Even fever reducers such as acetaminophen and ibuprofen should be considered optional. Your pediatrician will tell you that fever isn't dangerous. These medications should be *offered* to provide comfort, but their benefit isn't worth a struggle. Save your energy for when your child requires an antibiotic that might be life-saving.

Don't buy three or four different flavors of over-the-counter medication trying to find a flavor your toddler will accept. He will expect the same choices when it's time to take a prescription medication. For the most part, a pediatrician will be prescribing medication based on his or her assessment of which drug is going to work best in a particular situation. However, it never hurts to discuss the issue of taste while the doctor is writing the prescription. There may be some room for compromise, but don't count on it.

The pharmaceutical companies have spent lots of money trying to make medication palatable for children, and your pharmacist may have some after-market reflavoring tips that have worked for other families, but it is unlikely you will be able to improve on their efforts to disguise a nasty taste. However, as long as your child understands what you are doing, it is perfectly acceptable to flavor a bad-tasting medication with a *small* amount of food or beverage (no more than a half an ounce), but do not dilute the medicine in a large volume of liquid. It is very likely that the child will balk after a swallow or two and then nearly an entire dose of medication has been lost.

Don't try to hide medicine in food! This is equivalent to lying. The keys to having your child understand when you say "No" are honesty and consistency. Food is food and medicine is medicine. If your toddler discovers that you have spiked his food with medicine (and he will), you will have created a picky eater or made the one you have worse.

Unless the pediatrician has suggested it, do not use threats that the child will have to have a shot or go to the hospital. It probably isn't true, and threats like this can heighten a child's fear of hospitals and doctors' offices as well as erode your credibility.

If reflavoring doesn't work, you can offer a reward,

such as a piece of candy. Although I have cautioned you that reward systems generally run out of steam after a while (see Chapter 3), medication courses seldom last more than ten days. Don't be surprised if a reward doesn't work, and don't go hunting for more appealing rewards.

If reflavoring and explanations are unsuccessful or your child is too young to understand them, then your actions must speak for you. Forcing medicine into your child is never fun, but sometimes it must be done. For the first time or two, it is a good idea to have an extra set of hands around. It works best if the child is lying on his back on a firm surface such as a bed or floor. This helps minimize the wiggling and puts gravity on your side. Use a syringe (obviously without a needle), which can be obtained from the pharmacy or the doctor. Insert this inside the child's cheek and inject the medicine slowly. This positioning will prevent the medication from going directly into his windpipe.

If your child tries to spit the medicine back out, pinch his cheeks together between your thumb and first finger so that his lips purse out a little. It will be impossible for him to spit in this position. Wait until you know he has swallowed. It may take two or three minutes, so be patient. I know it isn't a pretty picture, but sometimes it is the only way to do it. The good news is that if you are swift and purposeful in your actions, your child will accept the procedure as inevitable and the struggle will be over in just a few minutes. It is very likely that he will accept the medicine more willingly after a few doses, if you make it clear there is no alternative. If the medicine goes down, but is vomited (not spit out) a few minutes later, this may indicate that the child is having a reaction to the medication and you should contact the pediatrician.

When administering eyedrops or eardrops, having your child in the horizontal position and an extra set of hands can also be helpful. It may make things easier if you warm the medication up to body temperature by keeping it in your pocket for fifteen or twenty minutes before using it. The sensation of cold drops in one's eye can be uncomfortable and frightening.

WHEN IS IT TIME TO STOP BENDING THE RULES? In most situations the question of whether or not to discipline your acutely ill child is easily answered. The bigger problem comes when he is recuperating. At what point in the illness can you expect your toddler to respect the usual boundaries? Eventually, you may learn to answer the question yourself, but don't hesitate to ask your child's pediatrician for help. For example: "Joshua has been on amoxicillin for three days and his fever has gone. Can I assume that his ears aren't bothering him anymore?" Off the top of my head, my answer is yes, but your pediatrician may want to

> Especially traumatic experiences such as the death of a grandparent or the unexpected hospital stay of a parent may necessitate some rule bending. It will usually be obvious when the crisis has passed, and that it's time to reestablish and enforce the old limits.

ask a few more questions before he gives you the go-ahead to return to business as usual.

There are very few pediatric illnesses that don't begin improving after a week. If you are still bending rules after two weeks, you should return to the pediatrician to have your child reevaluated. She will probably tell you that it's time to reestablish the old limits and begin using time-out again.

How to Say "No"
AT MEALTIMES

You may worry that your toddler will get sick if she doesn't eat anything green, but most food related misbehaviors aren't dangerous. However, they are annoying. In fact picky eating is such a common parental complaint that I chose it as the topic for my first book, *Coping with a Picky Eater*. If your child's eating habits are making you crazy, here are some of the basics to get you started.

HOW TO SAY, "NO, I AM ONLY FIXING ONE MEAL THIS EVENING." To cope with your toddler's eating behaviors you must understand that she can feed herself. It *was* your job to feed her when she was an infant, but now your responsibility ends with putting a balanced meal on the table three times a day. Once you accept this new role as simply a food presenter, you can sit back and trust Mother

Nature. It will occur so gradually that you won't notice it happen, but over the next six months your child will eat a balanced diet. I know it is hard to believe, but several scientific studies performed over the last seventy-five years have demonstrated that young children left to their own devices will grow and stay healthy, as long as they are *offered* (not force-fed) a variety of foods.

Promise yourself that you will only fix one meal for the family. As long as the food is cut into appropriate sizes, your child will eat them if she is hungry. Give up the mistaken notion that you can prepare a meal that will appeal to everyone in the family every night. Tonight you may serve a meal that contains one of her favorites, but tomorrow's dinner may not contain anything on her "A list." This is a good time for her to learn that she can't always have everything she wants and that a little overnight hunger won't do her any harm.

Begin by eliminating food from your mealtime conversations. Don't discuss who is or isn't eating what at the dinner table. This even includes praising your toddler the first time she tries a pea. Present a balanced meal and sit back. Talk about the weather, the neighbor's new puppy, or what happened at preschool, but don't try to talk your child into eating. It won't work, and it will create a tense and unpleasant atmosphere at a time when your family should be enjoying each other's company. People who are hungry will eat, and those who aren't hungry won't.

If you can follow this rule of silence about food, meals will become pleasant social gatherings instead of ugly food wars. It is difficult to keep quiet when your toddler hasn't touched a morsel, but in the long run it is a strategy that works.

The next step is to set some limits and administer appropriate consequences so that Mother Nature can work her magic.

HOW TO SAY "NO" TO OVERDRINKING AND INAPPROPRIATE SNACKING. Overdrinking is the most important, preventable cause of picky eating. It shouldn't surprise you that a child who is allowed to drink large quantities of juice or milk will feel too full to eat at mealtimes.

Limiting your toddler to four ounces of milk at each meal and four ounces of juice at each of two *scheduled* snacks won't interfere with her appetite. Allow her unlimited access to water and you won't have to worry about dehydration. If she refuses water, you know she's not thirsty. She just wants something sweet.

Her two (and only two) snacks should be scheduled in relationship to events she understands, such as "just after *Mister Rogers' Neighborhood*" or "just after we walk to the mailbox." If you aren't specific and simply say, "You can have a snack later," she will ask "later," which means less than five minutes from her last request.

Snacks and juice should be consumed at the table. This eliminates the habits of wandering around with a sippy cup, or nibbling all morning—two behaviors that contribute to picky eating at mealtimes and make your floors messy.

When you can't ignore repeated whining for extra

snacks or drinks, issue a warning and send her to her room for time-out as soon as she whines again. This is a safe and healthy consequence because you have given her the chance to drink water and eat at mealtimes. Keep in mind that even if your toddler doesn't eat supper, she can easily fast until breakfast the next morning without a snack. She won't starve overnight. Remember that this kind of behavior will be temporary as long as you stick to your guns.

HOW TO SAY "NO" TO BAD DINNER TABLE MANNERS. You can't expect your toddler to keep her elbows off the table and hold her utensils like a finishing-school graduate, but young children can learn that disruptive mealtime behavior won't be tolerated.

The rules are very simple. She doesn't have to eat, because like most of her peers, she probably isn't hungry late in the day. However, she must not pester or annoy the other people who are trying to enjoy their meals. Building castles out of mashed potatoes, and arranging her uneaten peas in a circle can be ignored. Whining, utensil banging, and throwing food shouldn't be tolerated.

She may get down from the table and play quietly in the room until the meal is over. (Remember, you have a toddler in the house. Meals shouldn't last more than twenty minutes.) However, once she has left the table, her meal has ended. There isn't any popping up and down from her chair to nibble or sitting on Mommy's lap and eating from her plate. Her next chance to eat will be tomorrow's breakfast.

If she becomes disruptive, issue *one* warning, and send her to her room until the meal is over. Make it very clear that she is going to time-out because she is misbehaving, *not* because she wasn't eating. You may be tempted to abandon this strategy after your first few attempts because it will create more disruption than your toddler's meal-time misbehaviors. I urge you to persist. After a few more trips to time-out, she will realize that meals are more fun, particularly since her parents have stopped pressuring her to eat.

Saying "No" at mealtimes can be difficult because you are worried about your toddler's nutrition. Check with your pediatrician for reassurance that your child is healthy and read my first book for the rest of the story. You will find it comforting.

Discipline and DAYCARE

If your toddler stayed home with you all day, every day, managing his behavior would probably be less compli-cated but probably more tiring. However, there are bills to be paid and jobs that must be done. Daycare may not be your first choice, but it is probably the best available option. Your child must adapt to a new environment or-ganized by adults who aren't his parents. There will be a different set of limits to learn and unexpected conse-quences if he doesn't. Out of necessity, daycare is probably less tolerant of misbehaviors than you have been. Your toddler will have an abundance of playmates, but the group may include a bully. Communal play is fun but it will require sharing, a concept that doesn't come easily to most young children.

If your child has difficulty adapting to daycare, his behavior at home may deteriorate. If he doesn't like playing by their rules and tries to buck the system, his disruptive behavior may become so intolerable that you are told to find a different daycare. Talk about unpleasant consequences!

Let's take a closer look at how daycare can affect your child's behavior and search for ways of improving communication with the providers.

THE UPSIDE: DAYCARE IS FUN. Most of the toddlers that I know enjoy the camaraderie and social interaction that daycare provides. To be brutally honest, your toddler is probably getting bored playing with you. He has heard most of your rhymes and songs hundreds times. His peers are much more fun. They are more agile and less inhibited than those old fogies he hangs with at home. In fact, I know some parents who continue to send their toddler to daycare even when other options become available because they realize it continues to be a positive experience.

YOUR CHILD MAY BEHAVE BETTER AT DAYCARE THAN HE DOES AT HOME. It can be embarrassing when this happens. Why does your toddler understand "No" when the daycare provider says it but ignores your threats as though you were speaking a different language? The answer may simply be that the daycare provider sees your child at a time of day when he is well rested and therefore better behaved.

A more likely explanation is that the daycare provider has already learned to set appropriate limits and how to follow her threats with meaningful consequences. She may have read this book before you did or stumbled on the right answers after years of trial and error. Swallow your pride and ask her how she does it. I bet she's been waiting for the opportunity to tell you for months.

IS DAYCARE MAKING YOUR CHILD MORE AGGRESSIVE? At least one study suggests that children in daycare tend to be more aggressive. This observation is controversial and certainly doesn't apply to every child. In fact your child may find the atmosphere at his daycare so intimidating that he appears more timid. However, it isn't surprising that a group of toddlers supervised by a single adult will compete for his or her attention. Many children respond to this competitive atmosphere with aggression or at least assertiveness.

If you notice your child has become more aggressive since he started daycare, it may be that the student-to-provider ratio is too high. On the other hand, it may mean that the provider is being distracted by a more demanding child and giving the rest of the group too little attention. Make a few unannounced visits and speak to other parents to confirm your suspicions.

The situation may be aggravated when aggressive behavior at daycare is tolerated instead of discouraged with appropriate consequences. Even if your child doesn't feel the pressure to compete, he may begin mimicking his peers' foul language and aggressive behavior when he gets home. What starts as a harmless monkey-see, monkey-do phenomenon may become a serious behavior problem if not properly managed. Later in this chapter we will look at the question of who is responsible for the management of misbehavior in daycare.

IS DAYCARE MAKING YOUR CHILD TIRED AND CRANKY? You expect your toddler to be tired when you pick him up at end of a day of active play. However, if your child is so exhausted that his arrival home is followed by one tantrum after another, he may not be getting enough rest at daycare.

Many toddlers still require more than two hours of midday sleep and if woken after an hour will be overtired and cranky at the end of the day. Most daycares provide a nap/rest time after lunch, but it may be too short, poorly timed, and inadequately policed. Even if your child's daycare offers an open-ended nap, staffing and space limitations may create an atmosphere that is neither quiet nor sleep-promoting.

If your toddler does manage to sleep through the hubbub of his earlier-waking playmates, he won't be appropriately tired at bedtime if his nap started too late. A poorly timed nap at daycare can disrupt your child's bedtime ritual, aggravate bedtime refusal, and guarantee that he is sleep deprived when he leaves for daycare the next morning.

If I were running a daycare, I would serve lunch at

11:30 and begin an open-ended nap at noon. With this schedule, the children who arrived underslept in the morning would have a chance to catch up on their sleep and the children who required longer-than-average naps would get enough rest and still be tired enough to fall asleep easily at bedtime.

If your daycare has had the same nap schedule for many years, they may be hesitant to change. However, if your child's behavior has deteriorated because he isn't getting enough sleep at daycare, I suspect there are other parents with similar experiences. Join forces and request a more sensible nap schedule. If this fails, it may be time to look for another, more sleep-friendly, daycare.

LOOKING FOR OTHER SIGNS THAT SOMETHING IS AMISS AT DAYCARE. Aggression and fatigue-related crankiness aren't the only signs that there is a problem with daycare. Your toddler may begin to object to going to the daycare he has happily attended for the last two years, or he may become uncharacteristically quiet and withdrawn. Toddlers can get depressed. This behavior may be a reaction to something going on at home, but first let's look at what might have changed at daycare. Start the inquiry by asking your toddler what's bothering him. You may be surprised how candid and insightful he can be.

Continue your investigation by visiting the daycare. Has there been a staffing change? Did your child's longtime provider leave or was she transferred to another room? Has the child-to-provider ratio increased with the addition of another child in the face of staff attrition? Has the arrival of a new child threatened your child's position in the group? Is he no longer the biggest, fastest, cutest, or neediest? Is there a bully in the class? Don't underestimate the devastating effect of the addition of one child or the loss of a favorite provider.

There may be nothing you can do to restore the status quo, but it never hurts to talk to the daycare providers. They may be unaware how changes at daycare have affected your child because he keeps his feelings bottled up inside until he gets home. Thankfully, most toddlers are pretty transparent, but your child may have already adopted a more adult coping style. Some personnel changes are unavoidable and your child will have to learn to accept them, but if the daycare can't maintain an adequate child-to-provider ratio or retention rates are poor and turnover rates high, you may have to look for another daycare where your toddler will get enough attention.

If there is a bully in the group, your child may not be the only one who is being intimidated. Educators and child psychologists have become increasingly concerned about the magnitude of this problem. You and the daycare providers will find an abundance of material on bullying at the library, on the Internet, or by calling the school department. While the daycare may opt for the easy way out by asking the bully's parents to find another daycare, his problem will follow him until he and his parents receive counseling in behavior management.

SEPARATION PROBLEMS: HOW TO SAY, "NO, YOU CAN'T COME TO WORK WITH ME." Most toddlers who have been in the same daycare since infancy don't exhibit separation anxiety because they don't know that not separating is an option. They have learned that another adult can comfort them in a crisis, even though they would prefer a parent if one were available.

However, there are situations when even your experienced and contented daycare attendee may object when you try to leave him in the morning. This can occur after a long weekend or vacation when your toddler has had unrestricted access to you. It was a lot of fun and it is easy to forget that the arrangement is temporary. Reality hits hard on Monday, and returning to work and daycare can be a painful grieving process for both of you.

Your child may also begin to balk at being left at daycare, if he feels things are unsettled at home. Children are sensitive barometers of marital stress and parental illness, and they worry when they feel the foundations of their support system tremble. An overheard argument, or a parent who is too sick to go to work, can be unsettling, and you shouldn't be surprised if your child is hesitant to separate in these situations.

Separations such as business trips or a parent's overnight stay in the hospital for a minor procedure can also trigger anxiety because your toddler's sense of time is still developing. Just a few days can seem like forever to him. Even after the absent parent returns, the worry may linger for weeks or months.

If your toddler has been home with one of you for his first two years, you don't need a degree in child psychology to know that his initial days at daycare or preschool are going to make both of you anxious. Most children find a comfort zone in their new surroundings within a couple of weeks and separation becomes a non-issue. However, some of us (and our children) are more anxiety prone and the process can take much longer.

Whether your toddler is dealing with separation for the first time or a change in circumstances has turned your previously happy daycare attendee into a tearful leg-clinger, here are some suggestions:

MAKE SURE YOU ARE COMMITTED TO THE SEPARATION. As long as you see other options to leaving your child at day-care, it will be difficult to say, "No, you can't come with me." Your toddler can hear the hesitation in your voice and will continue to protest as long as he thinks there is a chance of spending the day with you.

If you must work to keep your family solvent or if the degree you are pursuing is required by the profession you have chosen, there shouldn't be a question. Daycare of some kind is an unnegotiable reality for you and your toddler. Even though an absence of a day or two to stay home won't jeopardize your career, think twice before you cave in and stay home with your tearful, leg-clinging toddler. It's not going to get any easier tomorrow. In fact it may be more difficult, because he knows, or at least believes, that if he is persistent, staying with you is an option. Your toddler doesn't understand that you are running out of "personal days."

On the other hand, if your family budget can survive without your income, it will be harder to ignore your toddler's protest when you try to leave him at daycare. I am not saying that every parent who puts his or her child in daycare must be teetering on the brink of economic ruin to validate the decision. However, I am suggesting that it will be easier to manage separation anxiety if you begin by sitting down with yourself and then your spouse to explore your motives, goals, and short- and long-term plans. Hopefully, these sessions will simply renew your commitment to Plan A, but your child's protests may have prompted you to consider other options and career paths.

If the separation problem involves preschool rather than daycare, the issue of commitment is less sticky. While exposing a young child to a school-like atmosphere can smooth his transition into kindergarten, your child is just a toddler and there is no reason to battle the natural forces of separation anxiety now. Preschool should be more about having fun than gaining an academic advantage. Even if most of the children in the neighborhood started preschool when they were three-and-a-half, your child won't fall permanently behind if he stays home another year while he becomes more self-assured.

GRADUAL BUT STEADY SEPARATION. For your toddler's first experience with extended separation, the process should be gradual. Begin with a short visit to the daycare during which you stay for the entire time. Gradually, increase the length of these accompanied visits to allow your child to become more familiar with his peers and providers. After a few days of this arrangement, you can and should leave him at the daycare. Tell him the plan and promise that you will be back in an hour. The daycare provider can tell your toddler what group activity coincides with your promised return. For example, "Your mother will be back after circle time."

Repeat this pattern for another day or two, gradually increasing the time you are away. Even if your departure triggers a tearful display, carry through with your plan. As long as you leave and return at the promised time, these brief but painful separations will build the foundation for the longer absences to come.

I cannot overstate the importance of your punctual return. A broken promise will undermine your credibility, aggravate your child's separation anxiety, and set the process back to square one. Don't risk getting stuck in traffic or tied up at a meeting. For the first few separations it may be safer to spend your time walking around the neighborhood. Once your toddler is comfortable in daycare, he won't notice if you are a few minutes late, but for now it is imperative that you keep your promises and return on time.

Weaning your toddler away from you should take no longer than two weeks. In fact most families can complete the process in a week. Regardless of the pace you choose, always keep moving toward your goal. Separation will be more painful for both you and your child if you continue to waffle.

DEPART SWIFTLY AND CHOOSE YOUR WORDS CAREFULLY. Whether you are introducing your toddler to extended separations for the first time or reminding a veteran day-care attendee that your vacation is over, there is nothing gained by a long good-bye. The sooner it's over the sooner your child can begin getting comfortable without you.

One kiss, one hug, a couple of pats on the head, and a few well-chosen words is all you need to say good-bye. Avoid poorly defined phrases. Remember that your child can't tell time, and he interprets what you say based on his previous experiences. He probably associates "right back" with the time it takes you to go to the bathroom. "In a little while" and "later" are too vague and may fuel his unrealistic hopes of your early return. If you can't provide a specific time he can understand such as "after snack time," don't mention a time. Simply promise that you will return, and by all means don't sneak out!

Manage your departure using the principles you have read in Chapter 3. Bribes and rewards aren't going to make the transition any easier or your return any swifter. It all boils down to telling the truth. Instead of a threat there is a promise, and instead of time-out there is a positive consequence—your timely return. Once your toddler understands that you keep your promises as well as you follow up your threats, he will accept the separation without much complaint.

SHARE YOUR PLAN WITH THE DAYCARE PROVIDER. Experienced daycare providers have seen and heard it all before. Over the years they have helped many wet-eyed parents pry little fingers loose from their trembling legs. Their manner will be firm and reassuring. They will offer their lap as a safe haven for as long as it takes your toddler to take his first hesitant steps into the group.

Ask these individuals for advice in crafting your plan for achieving complete separation. Make sure that they know when you will return and how this has been described to your toddler. Of course they will want to know where you can be reached, but they understand that a twenty-minute spell of whimpering doesn't constitute an emergency.

The moment of separation will be difficult for all three of you, but the daycare provider has seen it before, and your child will forgive you when you return as promised. Moist-eyed departures will become a thing of the past.

LOCAL RULES AND LOCAL CONSEQUENCES. Just like your home, the daycare must have rules to minimize the chaos that accompanies toddlers wherever they may be. Activities must have a beginning and an end, and the safety and the feelings of each student must be protected. The number and complexity of the rules at your daycare will reflect the personality of the provider and be influenced by the mix of children it serves.

Your child may find himself in a daycare or preschool with a discipline style that is incompatible with his temperament. Persistent separation anxiety may be a sign that a loosely managed atmosphere is too rough and tumble for your timid and unadventurous toddler. On the other hand, the rules may be too restrictive for your inquisitive explorer and he finishes his day having spent half of it in the time-out chair. These mismatches are unusual, but they can occur despite your exhaustive pre-enrollment research.

If after discussing and negotiating the situation with the provider, the problem persists, you will have to look for another daycare or preschool that is a better match for your toddler's temperament. If the problem occurs again in a different daycare, take another look at how you are managing his behavior at home. Are you being consistent with your threats and consequences? Are your marital troubles more serious than you think? It may be time to consult a family counselor or child psychologist.

Privilege restriction is probably on the top of your daycare provider's list of consequences. "You can't use the sand table!" or "You have to stay inside during playtime!" are typical. These consequences are easy to administer and often can be linked with the specific misbehavior. For example, "If you throw the blocks, you won't be able to play with them again today."

Many daycare providers and preschool teachers like to include a little lecture with their threats and consequences. I guess they feel that it is their job as educators to tell a toddler that punching will hurt a playmate and it isn't a nice thing to do. You already know how I feel about too much talk when it comes to discipline, but when you are the adult in charge with a half dozen sets of ears tuned to your voice, a little propaganda about good behavior might make your job easier.

It isn't surprising that some daycare providers overlook time-out when they are selecting a consequence. I suspect that one explanation is that time-out in a group setting can be labor-intensive. Although you and I know that latching your child's bedroom door for time-out is a safe, humane, and effective strategy, there aren't many daycare providers willing to risk the image-tarnishing rumors that they "lock up" misbehaving children. Without a separate room for discipline, someone on the staff must be assigned to monitor the toddler sent to the time-out chair to serve his sentence.

Your child's daycare providers may have been hesitant to use time-out because they are unsure how you would react. Reassure them that it is a consequence you approve of and have used successfully at home.

Although it is important to maintain a dialogue with your daycare providers about discipline issues, keep in mind that it is their responsibility to choose and administer consequences for the misbehaviors that occur in their facility. To do otherwise is falling into the "Wait-till-your-father-gets-home" trap. Remember that all children, but particularly toddlers, respond best to immediate reinforcement, both positive and negative.

> When your child challenges the rules at daycare, his consequence should be served at daycare.

If your daycare providers consider the offense to be more than minor, they can tell you at the end of the day. It is up to you to decide whether further action is necessary. A short (five-minute) conversation during which you support the daycare providers' position is important for solidarity, but keep in mind that your child is just a toddler. Avoid the temptation to heap on an additional time-out or "grounding." A mild privilege restriction such as a half hour less television may be indicated, but for the most part the consequence meted out at daycare should be sufficient.

Grandma's RULES

When she's at home your toddler knows that you are the one who sets the limits and chooses the consequences. At daycare it is clear that her "Miss Rachel" is calling the shots. However, when you've made the eight-hour trip over the hills and through the woods to Grandmother's house, who is going to make the rules? There is no correct answer to this potentially touchy question. When your toddler finds herself in a different environment, she will learn that this means a different set of rules, but you can help her adapt more quickly.

It may have been thirty-five years since Grandma's hardwood floors felt the patter of little feet. Dozens of ceramic knickknacks have found homes on bottom shelves within easy reach of inquisitive hands. Toxic cleaning solutions sit unprotected under the kitchen sink and Grandpa's heart pills are lined up on the shelf above the toilet. Grandma's house is an accident waiting to happen.

After the welcoming hugs and kisses, make a tour of the house with your hostess to find the removable hazards that have escaped her pre-visit rearrangements. With the safety walk finished, review the schedule Grandma has planned for your stay. She may have packed each day with activities that run the gamut from visits to friends to show off her grandchild to eight o'clock dinner reservations. You already know that a day without a nap and a late bedtime will include at least one emotional meltdown and a flurry of misbehaviors. Politely ask if the itinerary can be made more toddler-friendly.

Although grandmothers carry a reputation for being loose-limited spoilers of grandchildren, this isn't always the case. If your mother/mother-in-law hasn't softened her house rules since you were a child, your exuberant and adventurous toddler will find it hard to have fun in Grandma's house. Everywhere she wants to run and everything she want to touch comes with a "Don't!" The best solution is to find a place where her normal toddler curiosity and energy is not only tolerated but encouraged. If the weather is good, visit a nearby park or playground as often as necessary. Is there a children's museum in town where hands-on exploration is encouraged? Even a trip to the mall may be less confining than staying in Grandma's "House-of-Too-Many-Rules."

The more likely scenario finds Grandma saying "Yes"

to poorly timed snacks, appetite-spoiling sweets, rowdy indoor play, and bedtime procrastination that she never allowed her own children get away with. While most new-millennium grandmothers shun the pleasantly plump, apron-wearing, apple pie–baking stereotype, "Number One Spoiler" is a badge they still wear with pride.

If your stay at Grandma's is going to last just a few days, take the path of least resistance and let her spoil your toddler as much as she wishes. She's not going to do any permanent damage to her grandchild with a little spoiling. However, make sure that she is enjoying her role. If you sense she is playing the martyr because she doesn't want to ruffle any feathers, help her draw a few limits and administer some consequences. Otherwise, step back and let Grandma rule. After you've been back at home for a few days, your child will readjust to the old limits you have created. That is, if you continue to consistently follow up your threats with significant and appropriate consequences.

If your stay at Grandma's house is for more than just a weeklong vacation, or if Grandma is one of your regular daycare providers, discuss your concerns about behavior management with her as you would with any other daycare provider.

Help her develop limits that will protect your child and her property. Suggest how she can do time-out. Lend her your copy of this book. Remind her that when she is home alone with her grandchild, she is the one who must administer the consequences. Waiting for you to get back from work or the grocery store isn't going to work.

Most grandmothers have as much trouble saying "No" as you have had. Support her efforts and remind her of the importance of creating sensible limits, making threats she can carry out, and then consistently following through. She'll appreciate the help and will be happy to brag about her well-behaved grandchild to anyone who will listen.

"He Hit Me FIRST!"
(How to Say "No" to More Than One Child)

Getting one child to understand what "No" means is hard enough, but when you are outnumbered, two to one, it can be overwhelming. You must set limits that are appropriate for each child's temperament, developmental level, and physical ability. It isn't as easy as refereeing a playground scuffle between playmates. When both combatants are your own children, you can't take just one of them home to defuse the situation.

There are times when you will be asked to determine guilt or innocence and assign consequences when you have no credible witnesses to the crime. In short, disciplining siblings requires the wisdom of Solomon. Of course any strategy for managing sibling misbehaviors is going to be imperfect, but I trust that after reading this

I understand that you may have three or more children who need to understand "No," but most parents reading this book will have two or less. To make this chapter more readable all the scenarios include only two siblings. The basic principles can be applied to larger families.

chapter you will have learned enough tricks to give you the upper hand even though your children have you outnumbered.

THE BAD NEWS: YOUR TODDLER IS GOING TO BECOME A SIBLING. After two or three years of ruling the roost, your toddler is in for what will probably be a difficult period of adjustment. When you bring his new brother or sister home from the hospital, you can expect more misbehaviors, tantrums, and general crankiness. While he will always be your first child, he must learn to accept the fact that he is no longer your only child. Some children make this transition from *numero uno* to sibling surprisingly well. They feel so comfortable with their place in the family and the world that sharing you with a new brother or sister doesn't upset them. However, most children experience some dark moments as they work through the grieving process otherwise known as "becoming an older sibling." It may take a few months or even years for your first child to accept the new family dynamic.

Here are some things that you can do to make the introduction go more smoothly:

THINK TWICE BEFORE ENROLLING YOUR TODDLER IN A "SIBLING CLASS." On the surface, a child-oriented program that introduces your toddler to the concept of becoming an older brother or sister sounds like a good idea. As part of their obstetrical promotional packages, many hospitals are offering "sibling classes" that they hope will help children welcome a new baby into the family. Unfortunately, these mini-courses can sometimes backfire and make the transition more difficult.

Regardless of what you do, delivering a baby and bringing it home is going to be a big deal. In fact it is too big a deal for most toddlers. Relatives come from out of town, mothers and fathers disappear for hours at a time, routines and sleep patterns are disrupted, and then the crushing blow—the arrival of a new person who intrudes on the territory that has been his for as long as he can remember.

New babies are powerful magnets, and everyone who visits wants to look at, hold, and talk about this intruder. The arrival of a new baby is a big deal, a change of catastrophic proportions for your toddler, and he wants things to return to the way they were, a time when he received all your parental attention. Even a well-conceived sibling class can overhype the arrival of a new baby simply because it's another group of people making a big deal out of an event your child would rather ignore.

Your soon-to-be sibling may be told that there will be lots of things he can do to help when the baby comes home. He may also hear that having a sibling is going to be fun. While that may be the case in the long run, the first months of siblingship are going to be rough. There is little to be gained by trying to fool your toddler into thinking that having a brother or sister is going to be one of the best things that ever happened to him. A detailed and gloomy disclosure of the awful truth about siblingship isn't going to help the transition either. The best approach is to orchestrate a few months of good old-fashioned denial.

THE "GRAND DECEPTION." What your toddler wants after his sibling arrives is something that he can't have—a rapid return to the status quo. However, there are several things that you can do to help create the illusion that nothing has changed with the arrival of the new baby.

First, adopt and promote the attitude that there is nothing particularly special about the baby. Resist the temptation to make unsolicited comments about her. Obviously, you shouldn't make any derogatory statements about your toddler's new sibling, but effusive observations about "how cute" or "how precious" her features and behaviors are may not sit well with a young child who can feel the underpinnings of his world shaking.

Enlist friends and relatives, particularly grandparents, to join you in this deception by asking them to restrain their natural inclination to make a big deal about the baby. Adults who understand the psyche of young children will do this without being asked. If they want to see and interact with the baby, they will approach through her older sibling. "Joshua, I hear that you have a baby sister. Do you want to show her to me?" If the answer is a silent "No," they will be patient and wait for the opportunity that is least likely to tarnish big brother's ego. Thoughtful visitors will bring a gift for the toddler and surreptitiously slip you the one they have brought for the baby when big brother or sister isn't watching.

Adopting this apparently ho-hum, just-another-new-baby attitude from the moment she arrives home is an important first step in giving your toddler time to adjust to the ugly reality that there is a stranger in the house, one who isn't going to leave.

OUT OF SIGHT, OUT OF MIND. By always putting your new baby to bed in her own room you will promote the illusion that she doesn't exist. If you allow her to snooze in a swing or car seat in the family room or kitchen, her presence will be a continuing reminder to her older sibling that he has lost his position as king of the roost. You may also feel compelled to do a lot of "shushing," which will only make the problem worse. In this situation, out of sight *is* out of mind.

LEARN FROM YOUR FIRST PARENTING EXPERIENCE. When your toddler was born, you were new at the parenting game. The novelty of the adventure and your inexperience caused you to spend more time with him than was really necessary. Feedings and diaper changes took twice as long because you were inefficient rookies. You spent hours holding him and chatting with him primarily because it was fun. You may have thought that these conversations were forming the foundation for his intellect, but it turns out that you would have probably been doing him a bigger favor by putting him in his crib to sleep during the first two months of life.

Don't get me wrong, you didn't make a mistake by lavishing that extra attention on your firstborn. If you had the chance to do it again, you probably would, but the situation has changed dramatically. Now you have a toddler who needs your attention, and if you don't pare down the time you spend with the new baby, you will see a surge in misbehaviors.

Learn from what experienced parents and pediatricians have known for years. For her first two months, your new baby needs only to be fed, burped, to have her diaper changed, and to be returned to her crib to sleep. Feeding, particularly if it is from her mother's breast, is about all the stimulation that your new baby needs until she "wakes up" as she approaches the end of her second month.

Of course few parents are so callous and mechanical with their children that they restrict their interaction to businesslike feeding, burping, and changing. There is always some chitchat, cooing, hugging, and kissing that accompanies these essential activities, and I encourage you to follow your natural instinct to express your affection for your new baby while your are tending to her biological necessities. Consider every minute you save through less-frills newborn care as another minute you can spend with your sensitive toddler. Your efficiency can create the illusion that, at least for the moment, an older sibling can have as much attention as he did before the "blessed event."

There are some baby-care activities that you can share with your toddler if he is interested, but his attention span may run out at inconvenient times. Breastfeeding can be a particularly thorny issue. Your toddler may be happy to sit beside you on the couch while you nurse. However, he may feel jealous and, realizing that you are vulnerable, choose his siblings' feedings as times to misbehave. If you don't have someone at home to distract him, you may have to send your toddler to his room for a time-out. Obviously, this confrontation doesn't make for enjoyable breastfeeding sessions, but eventually he will realize that his disruptive behavior won't be tolerated. Your baby may adjust her routine and prefer to feed at night when big brother is asleep and things have quieted down. This situation may force you to choose between getting a good night's sleep and nursing. A more extensive discussion of dilemmas you may face when you attempt to nurse your second child can be found in a book I have written for nursing mothers, *The Maternity Leave Breastfeeding Plan*.

CONTINUE YOUR OLD ROUTINES, BUT BE FLEXIBLE. Children in general, and toddlers in particular, find the predictability of routines comforting. As part of the grand deception that the baby's arrival hasn't changed anything, do what you can to keep your toddler's schedule the same.

Naps and bedtimes, including pre-sleep rituals, should

be retained. This may mean putting the baby down in her crib earlier than you had planned. Most children will be insulted if you try to make them go to bed before their younger sibling. It ruffles their childish sense of machismo. They're afraid that the rest of the family is having a party and they haven't been invited. Once your toddler is asleep, you can get the baby up for the feeding that has been delayed.

If your toddler has been attending daycare or pre-school, it's usually a good idea to keep this up, even though you will be at home and could take care of him. You and the baby will appreciate the peace and quiet that settles in while big brother is out of the house. Your toddler may prefer to stay home, primarily because he is afraid of missing out on something. You can help by reassuring your toddler that things are dull and boring at home while he is off at daycare. Some parents have approached the situation by cutting back the daycare or pre-school exposure (from three days a week to one). This has the advantage of allowing your toddler to enjoy the time at home with you without getting out of the habit of leaving you for a group activity.

It isn't unusual for an older sibling's behavior at daycare to degenerate with the arrival of the baby. However, if his behavior at daycare takes a serious downturn in the form of outbursts, continuous crying, or withdrawal, the solution is to allow your toddler to stay home for a few weeks or months. Hopefully, once he sees that his place in the family is still secure, he will be more comfortable leaving home.

Flexibility is also important when dealing with your toddler's search for attention. Whether your child has always been a "mommy's boy" or has favored his father when the chips are down, the arrival of a sibling can upset these preferences. Monday morning he only wants his mother to dress him, but by afternoon he throws a tantrum because his father has forgotten to invite him on a trip to the grocery store. Tuesday he spends the entire morning playing Legos with his grandmother, but in the afternoon he "hates" her and clings to his mother's leg. These changes in allegiance are to be expected from a toddler who finds himself in competition with a sibling. The adults in his environment must stay alert to his changing needs. Even though Grandma came to help out with the baby, her primary role may turn out to be play-mate for big brother, and then she must be prepared to shift gears at a moment's notice when the toddler realizes that he misses his mother most.

TURF WARS, WHEN CREEPER AND TODDLER COLLIDE. After a few weeks, most toddlers come to accept their new siblings. If your baby is healthy and doesn't require an unusual amount of attention, your older child will gradually realize that she really doesn't pose much of a threat. After all, she's either sleeping in her bedroom or eating. When she is awake she will laugh at practically anything he does.

This honeymoon of siblingship is short-lived. By the time his little sister is six or seven months old she will be mobile enough to roll or creep into the precarious tower of blocks your toddler has taken fifteen minutes to build. Your first instinct is to ask the older sibling to forgive the crime, explaining to him that the baby doesn't understand that towers collapse and that she didn't do it intentionally.

This explanation may work once or twice but it will wear thin quickly, because toddlers aren't known for their patience. Another alternative is to suggest to your older child that if he wants to play without interruption, then he should go to his room. As someone who still remembers what it was like to be the older brother to a creeper, I can recall feeling that I was always the one who had to make the compromises. Having to leave the social atmosphere of the family room if I wanted to play without interruption made me angry. It still is a reasonable suggestion, but if your toddler begins to grumble about going to his room, here are some other strategies:

First, you can begin to teach your creeper that with her new mobility come limits to protect her from the environment, and vice versa. At six months she may be a little too young for "time-out," but she can expect to be redirected as often as necessary to keep her safe and preserve the integrity of her sibling's toys.

Redirecting a creeper can be tiresome and the vigilance necessary to prevent every inadvertent and intentional invasion of her older sibling's privacy may require more time and energy than you can muster at the end of a hectic day of parenting two children. There is an architectural solution to the problem. By pushing a couch or a couple of large chairs into the corner of the family room, you can create a fort or play space for your toddler. This arrangement allows your toddler to enjoy the warmth of the family room while he plays. His toys are protected by the furniture fort, which he can climb into but his creeping sibling can't. Of course if he taunts and teases from his protected play space, he should be sent to his bedroom to play behind the protection of its door.

One variation of this strategy allows the older sibling to play in the playpen for protection. The disadvantage of that arrangement is that the creeper still has a visual temptation. I like the couch-in-the-corner idea best, because it is cheap and easy. It's the same principle I introduced back in Chapter 3: Use the things you have at home and can buy inexpensively at the hardware store to do the work for you.

UNWITNESSED CRIMES—WHEN TODDLER AND PRE-SCHOOLER COLLIDE. Crafting a discipline plan that works with two children who are old enough to know better is difficult, to say the least. Often, you haven't witnessed the infraction, and you must rely on the story as told to you by the combatants, neither of whom can be counted upon to give credible testimony. Not having actually met King Solomon, I will defer to my mother, the wisest person I have known, for the solution to this dilemma. She would have replied, "Send both the accuser and the accused to time-out." Her argument would be that identical consequences will encourage both children to seek a peaceful resolution on their own the next time a disagreement arises, regardless of who started the fight. Unless you are absolutely sure that there is a single instigator, my mother's advice remains the best I can offer. "I don't know who started this, but I know how we are going to stop it" are the words to remember.

THE 50:50 MYTH. When our second child was born, I thought that my wife and I should try to divide our parental attention equally between the two girls. By the time our son was born two years later, it was clear that giving each child exactly one third of our attention was not going to work, because our attempts at doing 50:50 with our daughters had failed miserably.

Each situation requires a reassessment of where you invest your parental energies. On any given day, one child may be sicker or sadder or more sleep deprived than his sibling(s), and you must be able to adjust to the circumstances. Over the long haul, you will discover that for one reason or another, one of your children always demands more attention than his siblings. In Chapter 3 we talked about the importance of understanding your child's temperament. When you have more than one child, they will have very different temperaments. The one with the more fragile ego or demanding personality will always seem to need and therefore receive the bulk of your attention. It may not seem fair, but no one has guaranteed that life is fair. You must continue to create the illusion that you are dividing your parental energies equally, but of course it's only an illusion.

LETTING THE FIGHT GO ON. When sibling rivalry gets physical and your children start beating on each other, you may be tempted to step back and allow the altercation to reach its natural conclusion. Letting them "settle it for themselves" sounds like a reasonable solution. On the other hand, you don't want to condone physical solutions to problems that could be solved by peaceful negotiation.

There is no one correct way to manage fights between your children. If you are a witness to the battle, you must step in. However, if you only hear the scuffle, you can pretend that you don't (see pages 61–64 on "Ignorance . . . Not Always Blissful") and hope that they resolve the disagreement on their own. But you must be listening carefully enough so that you can intervene when it sounds like one of the combatants may get injured. Once they discover you are aware of the tussle, both children must be sent to time-out regardless of who has the upper hand or started the fracas.

One of the most common scenarios involves the younger child (usually an eighteen- to twenty-four-month-old toddler) beating up on an older, larger, but more sensitive and timid sibling. "Mommy, Rachel keeps pulling my hair." After hearing this whining complaint from the older child for the fourteenth time in a half an hour, it may be tempting to suggest the obvious solution: "Give her hair a tug, so she feels how it hurts." However, a better solution is to praise the older child for his tolerance and introduce the concept of time-out to the younger child, if you haven't done so already.

STALLED Potty Training
(When and How to Say, "No, You're Too Old to Wear a Diaper!")

Although it may be appropriate to discipline a five-year-old for ignoring his bladder's warning signs, threats and consequences are usually counterproductive when it's time for toddler toilet training. Taking a two-year-old out of diapers before she feels comfortable with using the toilet can result in stool withholding and a serious constipation problem.

I'm sure that you have heard many times that you should wait until your child is "ready" before you begin potty training. However, you may be surprised to learn that she has been physically capable of controlling her bladder and bowels since well before she could walk. Clearly, we must be talking about an emotional readiness that may not come until after her third birthday.

If your child begins asking to use the potty or begins imitating toileting behavior, she is ready to *start* training. (If you think your child is on the threshold, it is okay to ask if she wants to try, but it is a mistake to badger her.) However, she may not be prepared to *finish* the process for many months. You should expect several frustrating stops and starts along the way. It is not unusual for a toddler to demonstrate bladder control and have a few good days or weeks and then inexplicably begin having accidents or beg to wear diapers again.

Although a thorough discussion of toilet training is beyond the scope of this book, here are a few tips that will help you deal with these frustrating relapses that can occur after you thought you were well on the way to toilet training.

First, make sure that this return to wetting is not a symptom of a urinary tract infection. This is very unlikely if you have a circumcised boy, but it is still a good idea to consult your pediatrician. Next, accept the fact that bedwetting is almost always a normal, but exasperating, sleep pattern phenomenon that will not respond to behavior modification or discipline. Night dryness will come with time, but that may mean many years. Allowing your toddler to wear diapers at night and underpants during the day is not inconsistent. It's just good sense.

Ask yourself if there have been any changes in your toddler's environment that could be distracting her mind from bladder control or making her seek a return to the security of a diaper? Is there a new baby in the house? Is there trouble at daycare, a change in work schedules, visitors, illness, fatigue, etc.? You probably won't find a cause because most relapses occur because your toddler has simply decided that the novelty of the potty has worn off, and she prefers the convenience of a diaper.

Begin by changing the way you present the issue. If you have been *asking,* "Do you have to (or want to) use the potty," you are offering your toddler the chance to give the wrong answer. Do you really care if she "wants" to use the potty? Do you really think she knows if she "has" to pee, and if she does have to pee, where does that process sit on her priority list? You already know it isn't very high, because she doesn't care if she wets herself.

A better approach is to *tell* (not ask) your toddler, "Before you sit down to watch *Mister Rogers,* I want you to go pee." If she says she doesn't have to pee, tell her that the TV isn't going to be turned on until she does. This is not a reward, it is primarily a statement of fact . . . and secondarily a consequence.

Link her trips to the bathroom to activities that are appropriately spaced (no more than two hours apart) and are ones in which she has a positive investment. For example "before we walk to the mailbox, before you go out to play, before you sit down for snack." Eventually she will anticipate the activity and initiate the process herself. This may take years. Every experienced parent knows to announce to the rest of the family, "I want everyone (regardless of age) to go to the bathroom" before leaving for a car ride of more than twenty minutes.

When you think about it, anticipatory voiding is the way you manage your own bladder. You seldom wait until the urge to urinate is intense before you start looking for a bathroom, because you understand the consequences. You have trained yourself to go to the bathroom *before* you go out to work in the garden, *before* you go to bed, *before* you leave the house to go shopping. Toddlers aren't good at this kind of anticipation, but this method of creating associations will work eventually. If it doesn't, in a couple of weeks, mutter a few bad words to yourself, and put her back in diapers for a month or two and try again later.

Another frustrating scenario involves the child who is ready to master bladder training but is hesitant, even frightened, about having a bowel movement on the toilet. This kind of toddler anxiety is extremely common and may be foiling your attempts at bladder training.

The solution is to separate the two toileting functions. Place your child in underpants and remind her as necessary to urinate in the toilet. Tell her that if she feels the urge to have a bowel movement (or if you can see by her behavior that she has to go), you will put her in a diaper (or pull-up) and accompany her to the bathroom (or stand outside if she would rather be alone). After she has pooped in the diaper, you can clean her up, allow her to flush the toilet, and return her to her underpants. Resist the natural temptation to ask her, "Don't you want to try pooping on the potty this time?" It may be months or years, but eventually she will do it. If you push, she will start holding back her stools and may start wetting again.

With this compromise you will have a child who is "bathroom" trained, although maybe not "potty" trained. "Hiding" in the bathroom to have her bowel movements in a diaper is certainly better than sneaking off behind the couch or under the kitchen table to go in her underpants.

The Velcro TODDLER
(How to Say, "No, You Can't Follow Me Everywhere, Every Minute of the Day.")

I recently spoke with a stay-at-home mother who was struggling with her two-year-old's misbehaviors. The frazzled woman understood time-out, but admitted that she was too exhausted to say "No" and follow up with consequences. She was doing an excellent job of getting her toddler in bed and asleep before 7:30. However, she wasn't going to bed herself until well after midnight because she was up doing the housework that she couldn't accomplish during the day with a twenty-five-pound child attached to her leg like Velcro.

This familiar scenario has its roots during infancy when, like yourself, every new parent is caught up in the excitement of observing and being involved in each step of her baby's development. The importance of this natural parent-child attraction has been overemphasized by some childcare "experts" who imply that if you don't spend every waking minute with your baby, he may not forge a firm and lasting bond with you. To make matters worse, you may have also incorrectly assumed that it is your responsibility to amuse and entertain your baby whenever he is awake. It's not surprising that some toddlers begin to believe that this relationship is a binding contract that will remain in effect ad infinitum.

The less demanding of these Velcro children demand that a parent remain within sight at all times; the more troublesome ones expect continuous physical contact. If you have one of these clinging toddlers, you know that it is impossible to get anything accomplished including going to the bathroom.

Before we look for a solution to overattachment, let's agree on two things. First, a toddler must be under constant surveillance. While this usually means within sight, many toddlers can be safely monitored with a parental ear tuned to hear that ominous thirty seconds of silence that means mischief is afoot.

Second, as the parent of a young child, you can't expect to get much accomplished on your nonessential to-do list while he is awake. For example, a twenty-minute phone conversation with your younger sister about her bridesmaids' dresses can (and should) wait until naptime or after your toddler is safely in bed at night. Likewise, re-painting the bathroom should be done at night when you can give this messy task your full attention. However, a parent should be able to cook a simple meal or spend seven minutes in the bathroom or five minutes on the phone making a doctor's appointment without a child attached to her leg or screaming in her ear.

Excessive clinginess may be a symptom of fatigue and the answer may be as simple as an earlier bedtime or an earlier (and possibly longer) nap, as in the scenario I described at the beginning of this chapter. A more expensive solution is to hire a baby-sitter to come into your home and amuse your toddler so that you can get something accomplished. Unfortunately, you may still remain his favorite playmate if he refuses to engage with his hired entertainer.

The ultimate answer is putting the Velcro child in his room for what could be termed a "safety" time-out. It really isn't punishment, and although it may eventually function as a consequence, your primary goal is placing your toddler in a safe place for a few minutes (ten at the very most) so that you can accomplish an essential task free of distraction.

For example, you are cooking spaghetti with your twenty-month-old attached to your right leg. It's a nuisance, but you are managing. However, it's time to drain the spaghetti, and the trip to the sink with a pot of boiling water is going to be risky with a twenty-five-pound ball chained around your left ankle. A three-minute "safety" time-out is the answer. "I'm going to put you in your room until I get this done" is all the explanation the situation demands. You needn't wait for your child to stop crying to end this time-out, because it isn't being used as a consequence in the traditional sense.

While most parents are comfortable sharing the bathroom with their toddlers, there may be rare occasions when you need just a few minutes by yourself. Use a "privacy" time-out. If your two-year-old isn't satisfied simply saying "Hi!" to the appliance repairman who has phoned to schedule a visit, a "convenience" time-out will allow you the four scream-free minutes it takes to describe the problem with your dishwasher and make the appointment to have it fixed.

As long as they are kept brief and used sparingly, these nonconsequential time-outs will not interfere with your overall discipline strategy. They are to be used strictly in emergency situations when there isn't enough time to issue warnings and threats.

Home Office RULES
(How to Say "No" to Toddler Harassment in the Workplace)

The fax machine, the home computer, and the Internet have made it easier for parents to work at home . . . at least technologically speaking. The advantages of being just a few steps away from your young child make a home office sound appealing. However, proximity can be a double-edged sword. Typing a proposal or talking on the phone with your most valued client with a squirmy two-year-old on your lap doesn't work.

After watching scores of parents struggle with the challenges of working at home, I have learned that the most successful were those who set well-defined limits of both time and space. And the earlier they made these rules the easier they were to enforce.

Your toddler will have trouble accepting the concept that there are times you won't play with her even though you are in the house with her, unless the arrangement is presented in concrete terms she can understand. For example, if the room you use for your home office has been off limits since even before she could crawl, she doesn't realize that joining you while you are at the computer creating a spreadsheet is an option. It's not too late to define an office space, but it must be clearly demarcated. A door that closes is almost mandatory. This is another example of an architectural solution to a limit-setting problem.

Your child will accept the necessity of physical separation more easily if you create and adhere to a work schedule that continues to give her frequent access to you and is predictable and linked to her routine. For example, your child will understand the reality of your home-based job more quickly if you *always* go into your office for an hour and a half after breakfast and two hours after lunch. She knows that the rest of the time she will have your undivided attention. (Obviously, these arrangements assume that there is another adult to supervise and administer consequences, including time-out, while you are working.)

My recommendation that you create rather arbitrary architectural and temporal limits for your home office may not coincide with the kind of flexible arrangement you anticipated when you first considered working at home. This may be because you underestimated the impact your toddler's needs for companionship were going to have on your ability to work productively. But now you understand that toddlers need and thrive in an environment with age-appropriate limits. You can still reap the benefits of working at home. It simply means that you will have to make basic simple ground rules that spell out a time and a place for work . . . and a separate one for play.

Filling Your BAG OF TRICKS

You have just finished the basic course in toddler discipline and you understand the importance of creating age-appropriate limits, making threats you can carry out and then following through on them. You also appreciate that sleep deprivation and a mismatch between your child's temperament and the situation are often at the root of his misbehaviors.

Now it's time to apply what you have learned to a collection of real world misbehaviors, many of which don't qualify as safety issues but nonetheless are annoying enough to make parenting unpleasant. While you can always fall back on the threat of time-out, there are many situations that you can defuse before they become full-fledged confrontations. The strategies I will describe with each scenario have worked for scores of families and are worth including in your bag of tricks.

THE TWO-YEAR-OLD NUDIST. *How to say, "No, you must leave your clothes on."* Learning to undress oneself is a developmental milestone worth recording in your child's baby book. However, some toddlers get carried away with the skill and disrobe at inopportune times.

There are two basic approaches. One of my favorites is the "Emperor's New Clothes Strategy." In other words, ignore your toddler's nudity. He isn't going to freeze to death or catch pneumonia. Even toddlers are smart enough to know when they need to put on their clothes to keep warm. Of course this won't work if the next thing on your agenda is a trip to the grocery store.

When the situation demands clothes, you can offer two (and only two) wardrobe choices. If neither option is appealing to your toddler, the next step is a swift, if ugly, wrestling match. It will take less time than negotiation and in the end you will have a child who is clothed and ready to leave the house. A no-nonsense approach to diaper changes should also be employed in the case of a squirming two-year-old who isn't fully potty trained.

The second approach is creating a sartorial scheme that is Houdini-proof. You may already realize that this is more difficult than most nonparents would expect. Putting overalls on backward, pinning zippers shut, sewing ties and laces onto shirts and pants can work, but you will need to stay one step ahead of your stripper until he decides that clothes are the order of the day. This is another example of letting inanimate objects set limits for you.

THE THREE-YEAR-OLD WHO IS FASHION CONSCIOUS. *How to say, "No, you can't wear your pink dress every day."* Many toddlers are very aware of what they are wearing, and a few become obsessed with particular clothes and refuse to wear anything but their favorites. Again, there are two basic strategies. One is the path of least resistance by running the washing machine daily or buying a second identical piece of clothing. The obsession will probably wear out long before the dress or the washing machine.

A similar strategy works when your child chooses what you consider an inappropriate outfit for a given occasion. Her choice is probably not inappropriate enough to warrant an argument. Just let her wear her raggedy *Bob the Builder* sweatshirt and overalls to your brother's wedding. Most of the guests have had toddlers themselves. They'll understand. (I have often thought of marketing a button for parents to pin on their toddlers that reads "I dressed myself!" It would be a perfect accessory for these special occasions.)

The other approach is to conveniently lose the favorite garment. You can always say that you sent it to the dry cleaners and that they lost it. In addition to solving the problem, it will teach your child an important first lesson about dry cleaners.

THE EIGHTEEN-MONTH-OLD WHO THROWS HIS FOOD. *How to say, "No, food goes in your mouth, not on the floor."* Three months ago you were high-fiving each other because your toddler could throw a fabric ball accurately halfway across the family room. Unfortunately, now he doesn't understand why pitching his half-eaten waffle on the floor receives a cool reception.

Food throwing is a sport in which the pitcher is given only two strikes. After the first pitch, you can return the food to his plate to see if your toddler is still hungry. When a morsel hits the floor a second time, the game and the meal (or at least that course) are over. Even if he hasn't eaten much at all, you can be sure that your toddler won't starve while he is waiting for the next meal. It won't take very many two-strikes-and-you're-out innings for your child to realize that there is a more appropriate way to signal that he has had enough of something on his plate or tray.

THE FIFTEEN-MONTH-OLD WHO WON'T STAY BELTED IN. *How to say, "No, you must stay in your car seat!"* Driving is an activity that demands your full attention. You can't and shouldn't be making threats and consequences while you are behind the wheel. This is another situation in which you must rely on your architectural and mechanical creativity for the solution.

Are there adjustments you can make to the seat to make escape impossible? Would an additional Velcro strap or two solve the problem? (Remember, that your solution must still allow for rapid removal in case you are in an accident.)

If your toddler unhooks the straps herself, you can cover her hands and arms with adult socks pulled up over her elbows. Then layer on a long-sleeved shirt so that she can't remove the socks. This solution will keep her precociously dexterous fingers out of trouble until she is old enough to understand the importance of staying in her car seat.

THE THREE-AND-HALF-YEAR-OLD MASTURBATOR. Some little girls discover the pleasure of masturbation before they can walk. For most of them it is a process that helps them to relax before they go to sleep, but some toddlers will grasp any opportunity they can to "ride" a pillow, stuffed toy, or upholstered arm of a couch.

Because masturbation is a normal and healthy activity when done in moderation, this is not a behavior that requires an absolute "No!" Begin by making sure that your child is getting enough rest. Next, offer her extra physical attention such as hugs, pats on the head, and sits in your lap, because it has been discovered that increased physical contact will decrease excess masturbation.

Finally, tell her that if she feels like masturbating (use whatever term has evolved in your family) that she should go to her room because that is the appropriate place. Make it clear that this is not a time-out or consequence for being bad. This is merely a statement of fact. The bathroom is for toileting, the dining room is for eating, and masturbation is done in the privacy of one's bedroom.

While little boys seldom masturbate, many of them enjoy crotch grabbing or, as one mother I know describes it, "rearranging their furniture." This is generally not a fatigue-related activity, but your responses should be the same as they would be for masturbation.

THE FOUR-YEAR-OLD WHO SWEARS. First, look for the source of the profanity. Hopefully, you won't find it at home. Are your child and his playmates being appropriately monitored at daycare? At the baby-sitter's? At friends' houses? Do what you can to squelch the source, but as your child gets older, you will never be able to shield him from profanity.

You can begin by telling your toddler, "That word isn't nice and I don't want you to use it." If this turns swearing into a game intended to get your attention, then ignoring the bad words is your next option. But this won't work in public.

When all else fails, profanity should be managed with time-out. I don't recommend washing your swearing toddler's mouth out with soap.

THUMBSUCKING. While thumb and finger sucking can lead to dental deformities in an older child who has his permanent teeth, it is not a habit that demands attention during the toddler years. Begin by addressing any fears, sadness, or incipient illnesses that may be triggering an unusual amount of thumbsucking. However, because it is a behavior that usually indicates that your child is over-tired, I recommend that you respond when it is excessive.

Covering thumbs with Band-Aids or painting them with bad-tasting substances seldom works. If thumbsucking is linked to a favorite ("transitional" or "security") object, make the rule that the object remains in your child's room, where she can use it whenever she wishes. The exception is during a long (more than an hour) car ride or times when an anxiety-provoking event is expected (e.g., a trip to the doctor's office). The same limit can be applied to a pacifier.

When thumbsucking is not associated with a special object, you can send your toddler to her room when you see the behavior starting. Make it clear that this is not a time-out, but merely one of those "there is a time and a place for everything" rules, and your room is the place to go when you feel the need to suck your thumb.

When thumbsucking is associated with an activity, in-

terrupt the activity. For example, if your toddler sucks her
thumb while watching television, turn the set off.

THE TWO-YEAR-OLD WHO WON'T LEAVE THE PET ALONE.
Most felines are clever enough to escape the clutches of
an overattentive toddler. If cornered, they will respond
with their own natural consequence by biting or scratch-
ing. On the other hand, a young kitten may be unable to
defend itself. In this case, if your toddler refuses to respond to your request to leave the cat alone, he's too
young for a pet and it's time to find the cat a new home
before the rest of the family has become attached to it.

Dogs present a more serious problem because their response to pestering could be a disfiguring or even life-
threatening bite. Even mature and historically placid dogs
have their limits and may lash out after one too many
pokes in the ear without warning.

If your toddler has ignored your warnings, and architectural separation with gates and doors is impractical,
you can try time out. This may not be successful if the dog
remains as a visible and tempting, albeit unwilling, play-
mate. It may be time to get rid of the dog. Obviously, this
step can be a very difficult one if you have had the dog for
many years. Sending it to stay with another family for a
few months while your toddler matures is also an option
worth exploring.

THE THREE-YEAR-OLD WHO WON'T SHARE. Except for a
saintly few, sharing isn't a concept that any of us accepts
easily. This is particularly true for a toddler and it is un-

reasonable to expect a three-year-old to share favorite toys with her playmates.

While you are waiting for your child's play date to arrive, determine what toys she is willing to share and put the rest out of sight until the guest has left. If your child is going to be the guest, suggest that she leave her favorite toys at home.

If squabbles erupt despite these pre-visit sessions, put the contested toy out of sight so that neither child can play with it. If this fails to bring an end to the unpleasantness, it is time to terminate the visit. Someone isn't ready for cooperative play or it may simply have been the wrong time of day.

Conclusion:
PLAN C

What to Do When Truth and Consequences AREN'T WORKING

You've moved your toddler's bedtime to seven o'clock, created a modest number of age-appropriate limits, and latched his bedroom door for time-out. There has been some improvement, but your toddler still isn't getting the message that you mean what you say. He continues to repeat the same misbehaviors and adds a new one to his repertoire nearly every day.

The solution may be patience. Although most children respond to consistent consequences in just a few days, the process can take weeks. However, if you have been struggling to be understood for more than a month and seen little, if any, progress, it's time for Plan B. Ask yourself these questions again:

Is my toddler getting enough sleep? An earlier bedtime may not have been enough. If your child is still overtired, misbehaviors will persist. Consistent consequences won't prevent your sleep-deprived child from being inattentive, impulsive, and accident prone.

Am I threatening consequences that don't materialize? Listen to yourself. Even though you are carrying out *some* of your threats, the ones you aren't following through on are damaging your credibility, and "No" doesn't have the meaning you intend.

Am I giving too many chances? *One* warning, and *one* threat followed by time-out is the solution. Too many chances drags out the unpleasantness longer for both you and your toddler.

Am I spending enough time with my toddler? Remember, your child is the one who defines quality time. Has your job gobbled up too much of your life? Are you distracted by other projects or personal problems? If your toddler is misbehaving because he misses you, even carefully done time-outs won't prevent repeated misbehaviors.

Are there problems at daycare? Have you visited your toddler's daycare lately? Has the staff changed? Has the mix of children changed? Your child's failure to respond to consequences may mean that there are unresolved problems at daycare.

Is your marriage in trouble? Toddlers are sensitive barometers of marital problems. Do you continue to argue about where to set limits and what consequences are appropriate? Are you or your partner depressed? It may be time to talk to a family counselor.

In other words, Plan B is *re*reading this book and giving my suggestions one more chance. If your toddler's behavior still doesn't improve, the next step (Plan C) is seeking another opinion. Ask your pediatrician for help in selecting the most appropriate consultant. She may suggest you see a child psychologist, a developmental pediatrician, a behaviorist, a neurologist, or a psychiatrist. If your community has a child-development clinic, you will find one or more of these professionals working on a team with specialists in speech, occupational, and physical therapy.

Your child may not be understanding "No" because he has a learning disability. The relationship between threats and consequences may not be as obvious to him as it is to other children his age. Although he speaks himself, he may have difficulty processing what you say. Your toddler may have an attention deficit disorder that makes his impulsivity and distractibility less responsive to your attempts at behavior management.

Your child may be depressed or anxious. He may be obsessive-compulsive or have an oppositional-defiant disorder. For many years pediatricians thought that these conditions did not appear until older childhood. However, we now understand that they can be diagnosed, and in some cases treated, in the toddler age group.

These diagnoses can be difficult and the use of med-

ication in very young children is controversial. If someone labels your child with one of these conditions and
suggests medication, consider getting a second opinion.

The discovery that your child has a developmental
delay, learning disability, or psychiatric disorder is a
mixed blessing. Obviously, it isn't what you had planned
and hoped for your child. On the other hand, now you realize that his misbehaviors were much more complicated
than those encountered by the parents of a typical toddler.
Uncovering the problem at this early stage also means
that your toddler can begin therapy before he earns an
undeserved reputation as spoiled or bad.

How to Say "Yes" to YOUR TODDLER

LET'S FINISH ON A POSITIVE NOTE. Drawing toddler-
appropriate limits and consistently administering logical
consequences will help you be an effective disciplinarian.
But there is more to good parenting than becoming profi-
cient at saying "No!" Raising a family should be fun for
both you and your child and this may mean saying "Yes"
in situations in which your first instinct is to do just the op-
posite.

One of the most refreshing qualities of young children
is their spontaneity. They don't waste time planning and
certainly don't give much thought to the risks when em-
barking on a new adventure. As parents you and I must

create some limits to protect them while they explore, but if we make too many rules we will rob them of valuable learning experiences and may stifle their refreshing sense of spontaneity.

If you can learn to say "Yes" to your child more often, he will be happier. You won't have to say "No" as frequently, and you will share in his joy of exploration and discovery, a skill that you may have lost as you evolved into a predictable and cautious adult. For example, you arrive home after a long day at work. You are hungry and tired. It's fifty degrees and raining, and your two-and-a-half-year-old wants to go out in the backyard and swing on the swingset.

You already know the consequences. You both are going to get cold and wet. Muddy clothes are going to have to be washed and dried. Dinner is going to be delayed at least a half an hour.

Your work-weary, logical adult brain says, "No." On the other hand, your toddler may not have had a great day himself. Trapped inside by the bad weather, he has already heard enough "No's" from his other parent or day-care provider. Why not treat yourselves to a bit of childish craziness, ignore your instincts, and say "Yes." Neither of you are going to catch pneumonia. You can choose clothes that will clean and dry easily. Your toddler wasn't going to each much of his dinner anyway. Grab a handful of goldfish crackers to stop the growling in your own stomach and go out in the rain with your child.

Two things may happen, and both of them are good. Within two minutes of going outside your toddler may realize this was a mistake and will be less likely to make a similar request again. On the other hand, you may rediscover the fun of jumping in puddles and enjoy some real quality time with your child. Even at his age, this could be an event he will always remember fondly. You certainly will.

Learn to say "Yes" to some of your toddler's risk-taking behavior. It will mean fewer "No's," and it will help him extend the limits of his physical abilities. Obviously, you don't want to jeopardize his safety. But before you tell him to stop trying some risky behavior such as hanging upside down on the swingset, why not stand nearby and act as a spotter? When he is old enough to play out of sight, he is going to take all the risks he wants anyway. Your repeated badgering now is not going to change his personality. Let him have fun and develop his physical skills. Allow him to follow his natural curiosity while you are around to protect him. It may be a little more work and will certainly require some extra vigilance, but learning to say "Yes" more often will make parenting a lot more fun . . . for both you and your toddler.

Index

Limits
  during bedtime, 128–31
  flexibility, 25, 139–40, 154, 161
  home office and, 203–4
  natural inclination to test, 34
  on newborns, 22–23
  united front for, 138–39,
      140–43
  unrealistic expectations, 25
Limit-setting
  the basics, 77–85
  physical. *See* Architectural
      Principle, The
  your child's temperament and,
      85–87
Listening, 55, 56

Manners, 30–31, 71, 165–166. *See
    also* Sharing
Marriage, quality of the, 45–46,
    172, 218–19
Masturbation, 59–60, 208–9
Mealtimes, 134, 162–66, 207–8.
    See also Food
Medications, 157–61, 220
Misbehavior. *See also* Behavior
  during bedtime, 129–31
  causes, 37–46, 96, 120, 218–19.
      See also Fatigue
  don't rehash, 97
  due to fatigue, 19–20, 25–26,
      31–32, 40–41, 72–77,
      147–48, 218
  due to illness, 43–44
  frequency of, 37
  location of, 33–34
  pattern formation, 22–23,
      34–35
  pattern observation, 28–37
  prioritization, 29–30, 65
  in public, 143–54
  of siblings, 183–84
  when to ignore, 61–64, 195

Naps, 40, 74, 126, 127, 134–35,
    169–70
Negative reinforcement, 56, 179

Newborns, 22–23
Nightmares/night terrors, 40, 76
Night waking, 131–33
"No"
  child's ability to understand,
      7–9, 219–20
  ignored. *See* Consequences
  to more than one child,
      183–84
  why it is hard to say, 17–22,
      23, 73–74
  why it isn't working, 22–26

Older children
  adolescents, 9–10, 41
  preschoolers, 9, 174, 193–94

Pacifier, 135–37, 210
Parenting styles, 36, 66–68
Parents
  arguments between, 138–41
  different perspectives, 30, 35,
      137–38
  inconsistency between, 4,
      35–36, 137–39
  playing one against the other,
      35–36, 138
  as a united front, 138–39,
      140–43
Patience, 63, 74, 217
Pets, 34, 211
Positive reinforcement, 5, 56,
    179
Praise, 60, 61
Privacy, 192, 202
Privilege restriction, 178, 180
Profanity, 169, 209–10
Psychiatric disorders, 32, 219,
    220
Public appearances, 143–54

"Quality time," 41–43, 127, 218,
    221–22

Redirection, 5, 24, 52–53, 111,
    192
Rewards, 56–58, 159–60

About the Author

A pediatrician for more than twenty-five years, **Will Wilkoff, M.D.,** is the author of three previous books, including *The Three Month Breastfeeding Guide* and *Is My Child Overtired?* Dr. Wilkoff lives and practices in Brunswick, Maine.